Being Santa Claus

WHAT I LEARNED ABOUT
THE TRUE MEANING OF CHRISTMAS

SAL LIZARD

with Jonathan Lane

GOTHAM BOOKS

GOTHAM BOOKS
Published by Penguin Group (USA) Inc.
375 Hudson Street, New York, New York 10014, U.S.A.
Penguin Group (Canada), 90 Eglinton Avenue East, Suite 700, Toronto, On-
tario M4P 2Y3, Canada (a division of Pearson Penguin Canada Inc.); Penguin
Books Ltd, 80 Strand, London WC2R 0RL, England; Penguin Ireland, 25 St
Stephen's Green, Dublin 2, Ireland (a division of Penguin Books Ltd); Penguin
Group (Australia), 250 Camberwell Road, Camberwell, Victoria 3124, Australia (a division of Pearson Australia Group Pty Ltd); Penguin Books India Pvt
Ltd, 11 Community Centre, Panchsheel Park, New Delhi–110 017, India; Penguin Group (NZ), 67 Apollo Drive, Rosedale, Auckland 0632, New Zealand (a
division of Pearson New Zealand Ltd); Penguin Books (South Africa) (Pty) Ltd,
24 Sturdee Avenue, Rosebank, Johannesburg 2196, South Africa

Penguin Books Ltd, Registered Offices:
80 Strand, London WC2R 0RL, England

Published by Gotham Books, a member of Penguin Group (USA) Inc.

First printing, November 2012
1 3 5 7 9 10 8 6 4 2

LIBRARY OF CONGRESS CATALOGING-IN-PUBLICATION DATA

Lizard, Sal.
Being Santa Claus : what I learned about the true meaning of Christmas /
Sal Lizard with Jonathan Lane.
p. cm.
ISBN 978-1-592-40756-9 (hardcover)
1. Santa Claus. I. Lane, Jonathan. II. Title.
GT4992.L59 2012
394.2663—dc23
2012014420

Printed in the United States of America
Set in Old Style 7 Std Roman
Designed by Nicola Ferguson

Penguin is committed to publishing works of quality and integrity.
In that spirit, we are proud to offer this book to our readers;
however, the story, the experiences, and the words
are the author's alone.

Being Santa Claus

For Ashley, Jayden,
and everyone else out there
who believes in the magic
and wonder of Santa Claus

CONTENTS

Being Santa Claus

INTRODUCTION

I TAKE BEING SANTA CLAUS VERY SERIOUSLY.
It doesn't matter what the calendar says; no matter where I am or what I'm doing, when children come up to me and greet me as Santa, as they often do, I immediately slip into character. I might say I noticed them being good, and (with their parents' permission) offer them a candy cane. My pockets are stocked with a stash of candy canes year-round because I never know when I'll run into a flash of Christmas cheer.

Even my car, affectionately known as the Santamobile, embraces the iconic role I've come to play. My bright red Chevy station wagon has the word *Santa* painted in big letters on both sides. The license plate, which also reads SANTA, has a lighted neon frame, and a bobblehead Santa Claus sits atop the dashboard, underneath a sprig of mistletoe hanging from my rearview mirror.

Folks who see me driving around or handing out free

candy canes in spring or summertime say, "Man, you must really love Christmas!"

"Not just Christmas," I tell them. "I love the *spirit* of Christmas."

I don't think of Christmas as simply a single day during the year. For me, Christmas happens anytime someone reaches out to another with love; when someone gives just for the sake of helping another fellow human being; when a child's eyes light up with the wonder of believing in miracles.

I learned at a very young age about the spirit of giving, and that one could do so on days other than Christmas. I was raised in a poor area of Indianapolis during the late fifties by a single mother who worked tirelessly to provide food, clothing, and a roof for me and my brother. Meals in our home typically consisted of boiled vegetable and potato stews without any meat. But once or twice a month, a kind neighbor would go hunting or fishing and stop by on his way home with some extra rabbit or fish to give my mother, usually long after my brother and I were asleep. Our neighbors knew of our hardship, and while they didn't have much to give, they wanted to provide a little protein for the growing boys. The next morning, my brother and I would awaken to a house filled with the delicious scent of cooking meat— a rare and welcome treat for us.

I didn't specifically gravitate to Christmas as a holiday as a child or as a young adult, even though I began to resemble jolly old Saint Nick at a surprisingly early age. As I entered my twenties in the mid-1970s, my hair and beard began turning white. By the time I left the U.S. Navy at the age of twenty-six and entered my long-haired, unshaven hippie years, I looked essentially as I do now—just like Santa Claus.

Even though people would often smile as I passed by, and children would tug on their parents' arms in wide-eyed curiosity as I walked down the street (*"That beard . . . that hair . . . is he really Santa?"*), being Santa Claus couldn't have been further from my mind. And so my younger years passed with little Christmas influence. Indeed, I had reached well into my mid-thirties before Santa entered my life in any meaningful way.

The beginnings of my life as Santa were simple enough. In 1992, I was living in Charleston, South Carolina, running my own safety inspection business. Early that December, I was asked by my friend Michael D., a DJ at our local radio station, to play Santa Claus during their annual toy drive. All I had to do was dress up as Santa and drive around Charleston delivering toys to children, maybe giving an occasional "Ho, ho, ho!" No big deal, right? But something happened to me that day when I put on that outfit for the first time. I experienced firsthand the mysterious power of the red suit to bring out the best in people. People of all ages just seem to become more generous, openhearted, and happy—even giddy—the instant they encounter Santa. He represents everything that is magical and wonderful about humanity, and I found myself slightly awed by personifying his spirit, even in costume.

A few weeks later, when I had to put on the suit again and save Christmas for the folks of Charleston because of a well-meaning DJ's radio prank gone awry (I'll tell you more about that story later), I knew that playing Santa was more than just a passing fancy for me. I'd enjoyed acting as a hobby and pastime for most of my life, and I realized I wanted to use that passion for spreading yuletide cheer—and maybe even delivering a few Christmas miracles here and there. My holiday rescue that day led to home visits as Santa the following year, and, as I'll share with you in the pages to come, my life as a professional Santa Claus was under way.

My grandfather once said to me, "Sal, if your preoccupation and your occupation are the same thing, you're a blessed person." And he's right: I am truly blessed. For the past twenty years, I've had the best vantage point imaginable from which to observe the enchantment of Christmas: behind a white beard and jolly smile. I've listened to thousands of excited children breathlessly whisper their innermost wishes into my ear, and I've channeled Santa's big-hearted kindness to soothe the fears of thousands more who cried (or kicked, or screamed, or, yes, peed on my lap) when they encountered the big guy himself up close. I've met grandmothers whose eyes filled with tears remembering the special doll Santa Claus surprised them with many years ago and eleven-year-old skeptics who discovered new reasons to believe. I've stood by the bedside of a dying child whose last wish was to become one of Santa's elves and seen Santa's compassion for a troubled soul renew her sense of hope. Again and again, I've witnessed firsthand the presence of Santa Claus delivering solace, joy, and peace.

Somewhere along the way, not only did I learn to play Santa, but I also learned how to *be* Santa. Sure, I may look like him (and I'll admit I'm quite proud to be a naturally bearded Santa Claus—no glue-on white beard for me!), but it goes way beyond just the physical resemblance. I've come to understand and—I hope—embody the spirit of all that Santa Claus represents. Santa believes that even the smallest child can make a difference, and he treats every one of them with love, dignity, and respect. He takes all of their questions seriously (even if they're asking about reindeer poop). He always shows up when he promises, even if he has to steer through a blizzard to get there. He has ultimate faith in our capacity for redemption, no matter how naughty we've been. Through his legend of stealth generosity, he teaches us that if you look for a way to bring wonder to others, you'll find it. In my everyday life, I often ask myself, *What would Santa do?* And I find that the spirit of the big guy himself always leads me to the right answer.

And now I'm here to share with you my stories, in the hope that they inspire that twinkling spark of Santa in all of us. I know the holidays can feel like a chaotic jumble of shopping and pressure to make everything perfect. But beyond the tinsel and glitter, and even beyond the whimsical legends of flying sleighs and midnight chimney capers, there lies something far more precious. As Santa, I've had a front-row seat to miraculous moments, selfless acts of giving, and beautiful expressions of love. My Christmas wish is for my stories to enable you to recapture the magic and wonder of what the holiday season is truly all about.

ONE

❄

The Mysterious Power
of the Red Suit

I DIDN'T SET OUT TO BECOME SANTA CLAUS. I suppose there was just something about my white hair and long snowy beard that naturally landed me in the world's most iconic red velvet suit.

It all began when I was thirty-six years old, not long after I'd settled in the charming city of Charleston, South Carolina. My wonderful new wife, Linda, her adorable daughter, Ashley, and I moved in together and set out to make a life for ourselves. Even back then, children would look at me curiously everywhere I went. I'd been asked the question enough times to know they were wondering if I was, in fact, the big guy right there in the flesh. I always smiled back at them kindly, but didn't really give the whole Santa mystique much thought.

At the time, I was happily building not one but two small businesses: one as a freelance safety inspector and the other as an Internet communications developer, which required a rather extensive array of equipment. At the end of our driveway, I had a special switchbox the size of a refrigerator with hundreds of telephone wires running in and out of it. Four satellite dishes of various sizes (the largest one fifteen feet in diameter!) sat in our backyard, and to top it off, an FM radio antenna jutted up from our roof.

My safety consultant business kept me busy during the daytime, and I dedicated most of my evenings to soldering together specialized computer hardware. My weekends were spent in the garage with the door open to the street for ventilation while I cut, sanded, and nailed wood together to make shelves for all the electronic equipment I'd built. Neighborhood children playing outside would watch this white-bearded, slightly rotund man doing all kinds of mysterious things. Happily absorbed in my tinkering and building, I didn't know the theories they were cooking up . . . until I learned from a giggling neighbor that the children believed *beyond a doubt* that Santa Claus had moved in down the street.

I couldn't help but chuckle. Naturally, Santa would need to take phone calls from children all over the world, which explained the complex maze of phone lines. And of course, it's tough to know who's been naughty or nice without some major high-tech monitoring equipment. Wood and supplies were piled everywhere for building toys. Plus, the radio antenna had to be for communicating with the elves up at the North Pole, didn't it? Ah, the imagination of children!

My metamorphosis into a real live Santa inched forward later that year when, in a random stroke of luck, I won a pair of diamond earrings in a local radio contest. One of the DJs, a friendly fellow named Michael D., instructed me to swing by the radio station to pick up my prize. We got to chatting and, upon learning that I was a local businessman, Michael asked me to be on his sponsored team for a charity event called the Charleston Winter Olympics.

"Umm," I said, not wanting to be rude but quite confused, "do they know it doesn't snow in South Carolina?"

"Oh, don't worry," he said confidently. "We make our own snow . . . a whole mountain of it. It's a really fun event, and I still need a few more people for my team, so we'd love to have you come along."

It was for a good cause, so I said, "Sure, count me in."

A few weeks later, I arrived at the site of the Charleston Winter Olympics, and sure enough, they had transformed a balmy southern November day into an elaborate mock winter wonderland. The "sled race" consisted of zooming down a mountain of sand covered by slick wet carpets (which was surprisingly close in slipperiness to wet snow). All the teams had to wear signature hats, and Michael had chosen red Santa hats for his team members. So there I was, zooming down the hill on an old-fashioned wooden sleigh, red hat a-flying in the wind. (You might see where this is heading . . .) After my sled race was done, I walked past a young boy who, upon seeing me in my hat, Bermuda shorts, and Hawaiian shirt, pointed at me and said, "Look, Mom! Santa is on vacation!"

As the sun started to set, Michael took me aside. "So, Sal, did you have a good time?" he asked.

"Sure did," I replied enthusiastically. "It's a great event."

He put his arm around my shoulder. "I always like it when we can do something for the community. Charity events are really important."

"I agree," I said, and I meant it. "I'm glad I could help out."

"That's great to hear," Michael nodded, and I could see the twinkle of an idea glimmering in his eye. "Could you come by the radio station next week? I have a surprise for you that I think you're going to love." By this point, he was grinning from ear to ear and bouncing like a big, excited kid with a secret. How could I possibly say no to that?

A week later, I was back at the radio station with a very cheery Michael D. leading me to a storage closet. "Now, Sal, I don't want to pressure you," he said. "You're free to say no. But we got this especially for you." Michael opened the closet doors, and hanging there, amid the usual storage closet clutter, was a bright red velvet suit with white fringe.

All I could do was laugh. "Mike, that isn't what I think it is . . ."

"Oh, yes it is," he said, once again grinning like a kid on Christmas morning. "The day I first met you, I knew we'd be doing this!"

"Doing what?" I asked.

"Well, every year our radio station runs a toy drive in December. Toys get donated to us, and others we buy with money that people give us. Then, a couple of weeks before Christmas, we drive around Charleston and hand out the toys to underprivileged children in the area. In past years, we just had volunteers drive over and hand out the gifts. But when I saw you walk into the station with your white hair and beard I thought, 'This year, we could actually have *Santa Claus* deliver the presents!' And then when I saw you last weekend wearing that red hat, I knew we needed to go out first thing Monday morning and get this suit for you."

"Well, Mike, I don't know . . ." I felt a little awkward. I didn't want to say no, but I'd never given out presents to kids while I was dressed as Santa before. "I'm not sure how it would work," I admitted, "or that I'd know what to say to the kids."

"Oh, that part's easy," he said, laughing. "We'll have everything set up for you. We have a red van that we'll fill up with toys. Half are wrapped in blue paper for the boys, and the others are in pink for the girls. We'll give you the address to take them to, you drive there, and people will be waiting outside with the kids. You'll get out and just hand out the presents. You don't have to say anything at all except maybe 'Ho, ho, ho!'"

I was still a little hesitant. I wanted to help, but I had two businesses to run and a family to support. "How often would you need me?" I asked.

"I know you're busy with your businesses, and we'll work around your schedule," he assured me. "Even if you get in only one or two appearances, it'll be a really great thing to do for the kids."

For the kids . . .

I thought of Ashley. My new stepdaughter meant the world to me, and Linda and I were looking forward to sharing a wonderful Christmas morning with her as she tore open gifts with squeals and whoops of glee. But what about all those children whose families didn't have enough to get them even one gift? Or the ones who didn't even have a family to begin with? I knew the kids would get the donated toys from the radio station even if I didn't do it myself, but what a difference it would make if those children were able to receive a gift from Santa himself. With that in mind, I agreed. Unbeknownst to me, my days as Santa had officially begun.

Step one was getting myself geared up as Santa Claus for my first appearance. I'd never seen a Santa outfit up close, but to my relief it wasn't too complicated to figure out. First came the elastic-waist red clown pants; those were easy. Then the coat; it was a little tricky making sure my long beard didn't get caught in the snaps! On went the belt, followed by the boot toppers, and then the iconic hat. And then, of course, the finishing touches: the white gloves and glasses. I was ready.

I'd love to tell you that when I turned to look in the mirror, trumpets heralded and the angels started to sing. But really, all I saw was just regular Sal Lizard in a bulky Santa outfit. I didn't think I looked all that much like Santa, but I figured it was probably close enough that I could pull it off.

Okay, I thought. *Here we go . . .*

❄

IT TURNED OUT TO BE A REAL HOOT DRIVING the red van around town. On my way to the various drop-off locations, the radio station would announce over the air that Santa was driving around Charleston, and anyone who spotted him could phone in and win something. Callers had lots of fun, reporting Santa sightings on this street or that highway. People driving past me would honk and wave, and I'd cheerfully do the same in response. I didn't expect it, but I was having a jolly old time.

The best part, of course, was the children. They would cheer wildly when I got out of the van and started handing out presents. And their faces! I'll remember forever those expressions of utter adoration. Each time, there was this electric moment when they first saw me—a jaw-dropping flash of awe followed by unbridled excitement. And to think I could elicit all that for a child. What a wonderful feeling!

At first, I thought I would just stick with "Ho, ho, ho!" but after the first few days, I felt comfortable enough to start improvising just a tiny bit. I asked some of the children their names, and told them that they were sure to love the toys the elves had made for them. My years of doing theater in school were paying off, as I became increasingly relaxed in the role.

As the weeks went on, I saw more and more how powerful an effect that red suit had on people. Everyone I encountered just seemed to light up when they saw me coming—adults included. They became happier, kinder, and most of all, more generous. People would do the most surprising things when they spotted Santa coming around.

It first happened to me one afternoon while returning from a toy drop-off appearance outside a supermarket. I noticed that the fuel gauge on the red van's dashboard showed nearly empty. Dressed entirely as Santa from head to toe, I pulled into a gas station at the corner of a major intersection to fill up the tank. I grabbed the nozzle and turned to open the gas cap on the van.

"Hold on there! Hold on there!" came a voice from behind me. Turning, I saw the gas station owner, an older gentleman, walking toward me as quickly as he could from the cashier's office. "Santa's not going to pump his own gas at *my* station."

"Oh, don't worry about it," I told him politely. "It's no trouble."

"No, no, no," he said, grabbing the pump. "Please, let me." As he started the fill-up he asked, "Are you the Santa that's on the radio?"

"I am," I said. "I'm the one who delivers the toys."

"Well," he said and smiled, "you do so many wonderful things for the kids, this tank of gas is on me. It's my Christmas gift to you."

I felt so touched, and I wanted to do something nice in return for this kind gentleman. But what? Then I thought of something. "I'll be right back," I told him.

I walked over to the corner in full Santa regalia and started waving to cars as they drove by. People honked, waved, and yelled cheerfully, "Hi, Santa!" A couple of cars even drove in for gas, which is what I was hoping would happen. I figured it could only help this man's business to have Santa Claus standing in front of the station.

I didn't know it at the time, but I would have many different versions of that experience in the years to follow. There was the time I was on break from my Santa-in-residence role at a busy New Hampshire mall. The lines at the food court were packed with hungry holiday shoppers, but the folks there sent me to the front of the line so I could get a much-needed snack. Or the time I stopped to get food at a drive-thru in San Diego, and when I reached the window and the gal handed me my order, she said, "Oh, and the family in the car in front of you wanted you to have these," handing me a box of milk and cookies.

And then there was the time I walked past two men outside a bar who seemed on the verge of an all-out brawl. I wasn't in Santa gear at the time, but I'd come to resemble Mr. Claus so much by that point that even grown-ups got that look of childlike amazement on their faces when they saw me.

"Is there a problem here, gentlemen?" I asked kindly.

They both stopped and looked at me. You could almost feel the tension drain out of the situation as they backed away from each other and relaxed their fists. "No problem, Santa," one said. "We're cool. I'm not going to fight anyone with Santa around!"

At the same time that I saw how deeply the icon of Santa Claus affects people, I started to notice that being Santa Claus was changing me in ways big and small. I suddenly felt as though I had to honor the "purity" of Santa Claus and not do anything that might tarnish his image. Prior to that Christmas of 1992 when I first played Santa, I had been a habitual smoker. But once I put on the red suit, I would not allow myself to have a cigarette, no matter how much I was craving one or whether I thought no one could see me. I simply did not want a child to see Santa smoking, even if just by accident. Pretty soon I would do the same for drinking alcohol in public, or behaving in any way that was anything other than above reproach. Santa is never unkind, or irritated, or even stressed out. As I interacted more and more with children as Santa Claus, I felt a growing responsibility to maintain Santa's unblemished image in their hearts and minds.

I never forgot my brief encounter with the kind gas station owner that day. That was when I realized that Santa Claus isn't just about giving out presents. He actually inspires people to be more giving themselves. Santa Claus is pure goodness, and so he brings out the best in people. He is a symbol of everything that is wonderful, hopeful, selfless, wholesome, and magical about humanity.

I began to wonder for the first time if it was more than a series of random events that got me into that red suit. Perhaps fate had given me my white beard and hair for very good reason.

TWO

❄

Santa Sal Saves Christmas

WITH CHRISTMAS OF 1992 BARELY A WEEK away, I thought my enjoyable stint as Santa would come to a quiet end. Little did I know that before the season was over, as a result of a radio disc jockey's prank gone awry, I would be called upon to save the spirit of Christmas for one special little girl—and the faith of listeners throughout Charleston whose hearts she had captured.

Her name was Fallon. Her father, a local business-man like me, advertised on the radio station. He owned a car repair shop and tow truck, and would drive around at rush hour helping Q95 listeners with car trouble. Be-ing a long-time friend of the radio station, this me-chanic enthusiastically allowed Michael D. to call his young daughter Fallon at home in the mornings, talk to her about Christmas and Santa and what presents she wanted, and then broadcast this adorable seven-year-old's commentary repeatedly throughout the day.

To end each call, Michael D. would try to phone Santa Claus at the North Pole to see if the big guy would talk to Fallon. But every time they made the attempt, they could never get through to him and would instead run into some obstacle concocted by the DJs. Meanwhile, all the residents of Charleston quickly became enchanted with cute little Fallon and hoped she would get a chance to talk to Santa Claus before Christmas.

Everything went smoothly until the morning of Christmas Eve, when Michael D. phoned Fallon for their daily call. It began with Michael D. asking, "So, Fallon, where are your parents?"

"In the kitchen," she answered.

"And where are you?"

"I'm in the living room."

"Is that where your Christmas tree is, Fallon?" Michael D. asked excitedly. "With all the presents?"

"Yeah, the presents are under the tree."

"So they left you alone with all the presents?" he asked in mock surprise.

"Yes . . ."

"Well," Michael D. said mischievously, "why don't you pick out one of the presents for you and see what it is?"

"I can't do that!" Fallon said. "I have to wait till Christmas!"

I was driving around Charleston at that moment (in non-Santa mode) listening to the radio. I figured that Michael D. would pretend to call Santa on Fallon's behalf to report how well behaved she'd been in the face of temptation, or something to that effect. But despite Mike being such a good-hearted guy personally, he played a shock jock of sorts on the air (whose ratings went up whenever drama ensued), so things went a little differently than I'd expected.

"Don't you want to know what it is?" Michael D. asked. "I do! Just tear a little bit of the corner off one of the wrapped presents and take a tiny peek. It'll be fine."

The next thing we heard was Fallon exclaiming, "Oh, my gosh, it's a beautiful sweater!"

Michael D. sounded shocked. "Oh, no! You opened the present?"

"Just a tiny corner like you said I should, so I could see it."

Fallon began to get a little upset, so Michael D. said reassuringly, "Well, Fallon, it's Christmas Eve, and maybe we can finally reach Santa Claus at the North Pole today so you can talk to him and explain what happened. We'll get ahold of the big guy today and straighten this out."

Here we go, I thought, smiling. I figured Michael D. was just setting the stage for Fallon's much-anticipated connection with Santa Claus. This was the big payoff we'd all been waiting for the entire week. Along with the rest of the city, I was eager to see Fallon's Christmas finally become the stuff of dreams come true.

Much to my chagrin, that's not what happened.

Michael D. proceeded to dial some numbers as listeners heard the sound of the dialing tones. A fellow DJ from the morning show named Cathy Lee answered the phone pretending to be the North Pole computer voice: "You have reached the North Pole. Using your touch-tone keypad, please enter the first name of the person calling." Michael D. read off the letters F-A-L-L-O-N as he pressed some numbers. "Please spell the last name." Michael D. punched in some keys without revealing Fallon's last name. "Now enter the zip code." And Michael D. punched in five numbers. "Please hold."

There was a pause, and then Cathy Lee came back on the line, this time in a more normal, albeit official-sounding voice. "Hello, this is the special operator. Is this Fallon *bleep* from Charleston, South Carolina?"

"Yes it is!" Fallon said breathlessly.

"It has been brought to our attention that you have opened a Christmas present before Christmas Day, putting you on the naughty list. Therefore, you will not be receiving any presents from Mr. Claus this year."

Uh, oh, I thought. *What are they doing?* This wasn't funny or charming any longer, to say the least.

"Hey, wait a minute!" Michael D. cut in. "We've been trying to get ahold of Santa for the last week, and we still haven't been able to reach him. You tell that

Mr. Claus that Michael D. is calling from Charleston, South Carolina, and I want to talk to him *now!*"

The operator replied officiously, "We're sorry, sir. We do not entertain these types of phone calls." And with that, she hung up.

Michael D. tried to offer up some words of consolation. "Gosh, Fallon, I'm so sorry. I thought maybe I could get ahold of Santa and explain all this. Let's see what happens tonight."

"O-o-okay," Fallon stammered. I could hear the quivering in her voice and could only imagine the waterworks that must have followed once she hung up.

Listeners felt shocked, even horrified. The switchboards lit up with calls from furious parents demanding to know why Michael D. would traumatize this sweet little girl and ruin her Christmas. Some demanded that he get off the air entirely. The ratings were sky-high, but the goodwill for Michael D. and the radio station was now anything but. The story actually made it to the local television news that night, which reported how this ill-conceived radio prank had almost instantaneously turned most of Charleston against Q95 FM. The radio station was so much a part of local culture that the whole thing put a damper on the city's holiday spirit.

Of course, no one intended for things to get so out of hand. The original plan had been to have me dress up as Santa Claus, drive over to Fallon's house in the red van that evening, and give her lots of presents from the radio station in appreciation for all the phone calls that week. The next day, Michael D. would tell everyone that Fallon enjoyed a great Christmas with a visit from Santa Claus and lots of presents.

But the damage had been done. Simply telling listeners at this point that Fallon enjoyed a good Christmas didn't seem enough to turn the tide of outrage spreading across the area. The radio station needed to do something extra special for her. Someone suggested broadcasting my Christmas Eve visit to Fallon's house, but few people listened to the radio on Christmas Eve.

No, we would have to do this Christmas morning and broadcast everything live. Suddenly, giving a convincing performance as Santa Claus became critical. I now had to save Christmas for a disillusioned little girl while thousands of people listened to every word I said. Talk about pressure! After all, I'd only just warmed up to the idea of playing Santa. Up to this point, I'd simply handed out presents from the back of a red van and spread a little Christmas cheer here and there. Now, everyone was counting on me to be a perfect and believable Santa Claus. I had some serious reservations about whether I could pull this off, but Fallon deserved a Merry Christmas. Besides, my well-meaning friend Michael D. felt terrible, and so I agreed.

I sat in the red van parked outside Fallon's house as the sun came up that chilly Christmas morning. I had butterflies in my stomach, silently rehearsing what I would say to Fallon to explain what happened the day before. This was a mission that required precision timing, and Michael D. and Cathy Lee had given me careful instructions. They would dial Fallon live on the air, and Fallon's mother would go get her daughter. I had my car radio tuned to the Q95 morning show, so I would hear the call begin. As soon as Fallon got on the telephone, I would then have ten seconds to get from the van across the yard and to the front of the house. At the ten-second mark, the DJs would pretend to hear something through the phone, so I had to jingle my bells exactly ten seconds after Fallon picked up. This was going to be close!

I turned up the radio to listen. Michael D. called, and Fallon's mother answered. "Just a sec, I'll go get her," I heard the woman say. A few seconds later, Fallon picked up, and I sprang into action. I dropped my cell phone on the seat and grabbed the bag of toys. Silently tiptoeing across the dewy yard in the wee hours of the morning with a sack of toys slung over my shoulder, I wasn't just playing Santa. In my being, I was Santa.

In the meantime, the morning show listeners heard the following: "Hi, Fallon. This is Michael D. I feel so terrible about what happened yesterday. Did you get anything for Christmas? Did the big guy leave you anything?"

"No," she said sadly. "He didn't leave me anything."

Cathy Lee started scolding Michael D. for being such a bad person, and then I reached the count of ten. I started jingling some bells outside the house as loudly as I could. The sound was barely audible to listeners, but Fallon could hear it, and Cathy Lee's stopwatch had reached ten seconds, too. So she stopped her scolding of Michael D. and said, "Wait . . . Fallon, do you hear something? What's that noise? Are those bells?"

Michael D. chimed in, "Yeah! I think I hear them, too! Fallon, is someone outside?"

And then I let out with a loud and jolly, "Ho, ho, ho!" Cathy Lee told Fallon to open the front door to see who it was. (Fallon's parents had been told I'd be coming, so both of them were watching and filming the whole thing.)

"Oh my gosh! It's Santa!" Fallon shouted into the phone.

"Hello there, Fallon," I said to her, smiling and using my deep Santa voice. She was a little bit of a thing, not much taller than my waist, standing there astonished in her yellow bunny pajamas with the cordless phone in her hand. "Good morning and Merry Christmas! May I come in?"

"Sure!" Fallon let me in. I said hello to her parents and then got down on one knee, speaking loudly enough so that radio listeners could hear me through the telephone speaker, although at that moment, for me at least, only Fallon really mattered.

"I wanted to come here in person to apologize to you, Fallon. The North Pole operator got it wrong. I reviewed the case personally—even though I was so busy—because I knew what a good little girl you've been. So I checked with the elves, and they assured me that it was Michael D. who told you to do this. It wasn't your fault." I started opening my bag of presents. "Now, I could have just left your presents under the tree, but I wanted to come here this morning so that I could apologize to you in person for the whole mix-up and give you all these special presents."

"These are all for *me*???" Fallon's eyes opened wide as she looked into the huge bag.

"They sure are," I said. Realizing that Fallon was still holding the telephone in her hand, I asked, "By the way, Fallon, who are you on the phone with?"

"Michael D.," she said.

"Well, ask Michael D. what he got in *his* stocking this Christmas."

She did, and Michael D. said glumly, "I got a lump of coal in my stocking. Santa told me that I was really bad."

"That's right," I said. "Michael D. is going to have to work extra hard this next year to get off Santa's naughty list." I handed the bag of presents to Fallon's parents. "Why don't you put those under the tree and Fallon can open her gifts . . ."

Fallon ran over to the other side of the room and

started ripping off the wrapping paper as fast as she could, telling Michael D. and Cathy Lee about all the great toys she opened. That's when I noticed Fallon was no longer paying attention to me because her back was turned. So as quietly as I could, I slipped out of the house and hurried back to the van. Once there, with the cell phone line still open, I let Cathy Lee know that I had left the house.

I turned up the radio to hear Cathy Lee, who was still on the line with Fallon, ask, "Hey, Fallon, is it okay if we interview Santa?"

I heard a brief pause of silence, and then Fallon gasped, "He's gone!"

"He's *gone*?" Cathy Lee repeated, in mock surprise.

"Yeah. I guess once his toys are delivered, he's got no reason to hang around."

As I drove back to the radio station shortly after 7:00 A.M., I listened to caller after caller phoning in to say, "Michael D., you've redeemed yourself," or, "I was so angry at you yesterday, but today you've helped that little girl believe in Christmas again. I forgive you." And, most gratifying for me, "I loved hearing Santa visit Fallon and make her so happy. That was exactly the kind of Christmas spirit we needed."

As I drove home that Christmas morning to my waiting family, listening to dozens more happy callers, I felt a real sense of accomplishment. I'd made a difference in the world, even if just a small one. It's hard to describe, really, but I think this is something we've all felt whenever we do something from the heart, with the pure intention of making someone else happy.

For my efforts, the radio station let me keep the red Santa Claus suit. But I had something even more valuable: the memory of the look on little Fallon's face that Christmas morning. For her, the experience was simply joy. But for me, that moment of seeing her eyes light up as she went from despair to delight was life-changing. I suddenly felt wistful about hanging up my Santa suit at the end of the season. I wanted to be able to recapture that magical moment when Fallon opened the door and saw me, and do it every Christmas from now on.

You see, the world can be a topsy-turvy place—as we all know. Even the best-laid plans can go awry, disappointments happen, and conflicts and bitterness arise. But at Christmastime, I realized, the world *wants* to put the strife and cynicism on hold in the name of goodwill and peace on earth. Folks need to feel that Christmas spirit, just like that one caller said. And if I could help people do that just by being Santa and delivering a few much-needed Christmas miracles now and then . . . well, by golly, that's just what I was going to do.

THREE

❄

Santa on the Spot

I DIDN'T GET EVERYTHING RIGHT AS SANTA IN the beginning. Oh, not by a long shot! I made plenty of mistakes in those early days, not the least of which was learning how to answer those oh-so-tricky Christmas questions from children.

Stage two of my transformation into a real live Santa came nearly a year after my experience with Fallon. Out of the blue, I received a phone call from a stranger. "Hi, you don't know me, but my name is Dale," he said. "I got your number from the radio station. They said you were the person who played Santa Claus for them last year."

"Yes, that's correct," I said, not quite sure where this was heading. But I hadn't forgotten my tiny wish from last year to somehow re-create that Santa magic, so I was keen to hear what came next.

"My wife and I live in Charleston, and we have three kids. We were wondering if you'd be willing to come to our house as Santa Claus and hand out some toys to them. We would pay you for your time, of course."

"Well, it would have to be in the evening," I said. "I work during the day."

"Oh, that's fine," he assured me. "Their bedtime isn't until 8:30. How much do you charge?"

Charge? The idea had never occurred to me. The real Santa doesn't charge for anything, of course. Should I? There must be professional Santas, I supposed, but I certainly didn't see myself that way. Plus, it seemed almost ridiculous to me to get paid to make children happy.

"I'll tell you what," I said. "If you make a donation to a children's Christmas charity, as long as you show me the receipt, that'll be fine."

"Are you sure? We're happy to pay you."

"Oh, I'm sure," I answered. "It's Christmas, after all."

So we set up a plan. I would arrive at 7:00 P.M. and knock on the door. The father would answer and hand me a bag of presents as I came in. Then he would bring me to the living room to say, "Look who's here!" I'd walk in and hand out gifts, and the kids would get all excited. It would be easy . . . or so I thought.

When the father answered the door, he put a finger to his lips to shush me as he led me down a short hallway to a closet. He opened the door and pulled down a bag of wrapped presents from the top shelf.

Oops, I thought. I'd already made my first mistake: I didn't bring an authentic-looking Santa sack with me. The bag that the man handed me was a big plastic one with a recognizable store's name written on it in large letters. Santa wouldn't be carrying a shopping bag with him—Christmas miracles don't arrive via retail express! I made a mental note to get myself a real Santa sack if I ever did another home visit.

I walked into the living room to find three young children in their pajamas. Sure enough, when I entered the room, the oldest boy spied the bag right away. "Why do you have a bag from a store?" he asked suspiciously. Mistake number two: Never underestimate the observational powers of children. They don't miss a thing!

Good question, kiddo. Okay, think, Sal . . . think. Why would Santa have a bag from a store? I thought about Ashley. What would Linda and I say to her to keep her belief in the Santa legend alive? The year before, I'd done a little improvising as Santa while driving around town in the radio station van, but this was a whole other level. I looked around the room and down into the bag of brightly wrapped gifts with their ribbons and bows, desperate to find some inspiration.

Then I got it.

"Ho, ho, ho!" I bellowed. "Santa wanted to make sure to get here before your bedtime tonight, which I know is 8:30, so I grabbed the first bag I could find.

Wouldn't you know, it turned out to be a bag the elves use to collect scraps of wrapping paper!"

"How did you know our bedtime is 8:30?" the boy asked, slightly mollified.

"Santa has his ways," I said with a wink.

Phew! That seemed to have worked, thank goodness. I handed out the presents, which the kids quickly opened. Then they looked over at me. *Okay, what should I do next?*

I suggested we sing a few Christmas songs, which they enjoyed, and then we took a few photos like I'd seen Santas in shopping malls do. Still feeling a little awkward and not knowing how long they expected me to stay, I heard the mother asking me if I'd like to have something to eat. The family had already finished dinner, but they had some leftovers, and Mom was eager to make up a plate for me. "Really, Santa, it's no trouble. Would you like some?"

Five pairs of eyes stared at me, waiting for my answer. I certainly didn't want to offend this family by refusing their generous offer. With more time to consider the situation (or experience under my Santa belt), I would have politely declined. But I felt put on the spot for a quick answer, so before I knew it, I replied, "Sure, I'd love some. Thank you so much."

Mistake number three.

As I sat there eating in front of the entire family, I felt

incredibly uncomfortable. The real Santa is a mythical icon—he doesn't stay for dinner! He comes in the middle of the night and, at most, grabs a few cookies off a plate and washes them down with a glass of milk. I realized that while in the red suit, I'd have to take care not to break character. Santa meant too much to people to see him do mundane things. Later on, I didn't use a cell phone in public while dressed as Santa, or refer to my wife as anything other than Mrs. Claus. And I certainly didn't sit at a table and polish off a plate of meatloaf and potatoes!

I'd ultimately learn from this mistake, but that night, I was stuck. As I worked my way through a full dinner, the children took the opportunity to ask me all sorts of questions. After a few more Christmas seasons, I learned to field these kinds of questions with ease. But that night, I might as well have been a parent caught putting presents under the tree, fumbling for an explanation.

"Santa, why didn't I get the big-girl bicycle I asked you for?" asked the little girl, who appeared to be all of four years old.

Why indeed? Having a child of my own right around her age (and of course being a professional safety inspector), I had my own thoughts on why a bicycle might not be a good idea just yet, but that wasn't for me to say. So I stayed vague. "I'll have to check my records on that one and get back to you."

Then the middle child, a boy, piped in with, "Can I get a video game next year?"

Praying this wasn't breaking some family code of theirs regarding video games, I said, "Well, if you're good, you might get one."

"How good?" he wanted to know.

"Umm . . . *really* good?" I answered. I was feeling my way through this, so it came out more like a question.

Thankfully, the oldest boy tossed out another question before his brother could interrogate me further. Wow, they were relentless! Once again trying to crack the mystery of Santa, he said, "Hey, where's your reindeer and sleigh?"

Okay, now this one I could answer! My mind suddenly leapt to the scene in *Miracle on 34th Street* where Santa is in the courtroom and they bring in a reindeer and tell him to make it fly to prove he's Santa Claus. Remembering Santa's answer in the movie, I said a hearty, "Ho, ho, ho! Everyone knows that reindeer can only fly on Christmas Eve." Phew, dodged another one!

If I stayed much longer, who knows what these kids would be asking next. So I quickly finished eating and got up from the table. I thanked their mom for the wonderful meal and said, "Well, it's getting close to Christmas, and Santa has to go back to the North Pole. Merry Christmas, everyone!"

And off I went into the December night.

❄

IT'S BEEN TWENTY YEARS SINCE THAT HOME
visit. It was the first of many, so I've had lots of time
and chances to perfect my answers. During an unexpected Santa Claus moment at a U-Haul rental facility several years later, I figured out how to answer the
all-too-common "Why didn't I get the [insert inappropriate gift here] I asked you for?"

As I was waiting in line at the counter, I felt a pair of
eyes on my back and turned to see a boy of about eight
staring at me. I gave him a friendly smile and subtle
wave, but the boy had a look on his face that I've come
to know well. He knew that he'd cornered Santa, and
he had an important matter to discuss.

"I didn't get the BB gun I asked you for," he said
bluntly.

Ah. An unhappy customer. "Oh, well, you've got to
be *really* good to get a gift like that."

"But I *have* been good!" he said with obvious indig-
nation. His voice carried that certain challenge in it
that children can muster so well.

"Are you sure? Were you completely good *all* the
time?" I asked, hoping he'd admit to doing something
naughty at some point so I could get myself (and Santa
Claus) out of trouble. I glanced over at his parents who
were watching with amusement from across the room

as their son grilled Santa, silently praying they'd come over and lend me a hand, but no luck.

"Sure I'm sure!" he demanded. "I tried extra hard to be good all the time so you'd bring me a BB gun. And you should *know* that I was good all the time! You watch me—it says so in the song!"

It seemed as though I was being cross-examined on the witness stand by an accomplished attorney. I quickly realized that the old standby of "You've got to be really good" wouldn't work this time, and I needed to think of another way of explaining why this little boy hadn't gotten the BB gun he so desperately wanted. Even more than that, my answer had to make sense to a child and not break any of the established "rules" of Santa Claus, which included, most of all, that good children get what they want for Christmas.

I was getting a little flustered. How could I possibly explain to this boy why his parents hadn't given him a BB gun, for goodness' sake?

Then it hit me. Not only did I suddenly have the answer, but it seemed so obvious that it felt almost as if I'd always known this fact and had only just remembered it.

I got down on one knee and looked the little boy right in the eye. "Okay, let me tell you something really important about deciding which presents to deliver to little boys and girls. You see, Santa would never give you something that your parents wouldn't want you to have or didn't think you were ready for. Many times, parents will contact Santa saying that they know their son wants a BB gun, but they're worried that he might hurt himself with it because he's so young. Or Santa will get an email saying, 'My daughter is too little to have a cell phone. She might lose it or break it, even if she doesn't mean to. We want her to learn to be more responsible and become a little older before she gets one.'"

The little boy hung on every word as I continued. "If I went against the wishes of your parents, they might not invite me into your house the next year. And that wouldn't be any fun, would it?"

"It'd be awful!" he agreed.

"And imagine if, heaven forbid, you got hurt playing with a toy I'd given you. I'd feel terrible! So what I do is listen carefully to what children want for Christmas to give me a good idea of the kinds of toys they like. Then I try to give them appropriate presents that are as close as possible to what the children asked for."

He nodded. "Okay, I get it."

"So let me ask you something," I continued. "Did you still have a good Christmas, even though you didn't get everything you wanted?"

He thought for a second. "Yeah . . ."

"Well, that's what's important," I said with a smile.

"But I really want a BB gun! What should I do?" he pleaded, hoping to get some advice from the big guy himself on how to work the system.

Another big question: How do I earn the toy I want? The boy had obviously been giving this a lot of thought.

This question was easy, though. "Part of what you need to do is show your parents that you're ready for something like that. Make sure you do your chores and act responsibly. And when your mom or dad thinks you're ready for a BB gun, one of them will get in touch with me and let me know. Does that sound fair?"

"Yeah," he said.

By this point, the boy's father had wandered over. As the dad heard me finishing up, I saw him smile and give me the thumbs-up, letting me know I'd done well.

I've used this same answer in various forms countless times over the years. In fact, I've actually elaborated on it a bit, like when I encounter children with a really long wish list of toys—or ones that want to know why they didn't get everything they asked for last year. I tell them that if Santa gave them *everything* on their list, he would be spoiling them. And parents don't like to have spoiled children any more than they like to have spoiled milk. So Santa makes sure to give just enough presents without giving too much, so that children and their parents are both happy. If children knew that they would always get everything on their Christmas list, then they would never be surprised on Christmas morning, and Santa loves to surprise children.

These days, I usually finish off by telling children the following thing, which always makes them giggle:

"You know, I've never had any child call me up at the North Pole and say, 'I don't like the present you gave me! Come back here and get it, and give me what I asked for!' Not that I ever would, of course."

And you know what? Almost all children accept that. When you think about it, Santa has some very ambiguous rules. So when an adult, or Santa himself, explains more clearly how things work when asking for and getting presents—just like that little boy at the U-Haul counter—most kids will say, "Yeah, I get it."

✳

AND THEN, OF COURSE, COMES THE BIGGEST question of all: "Are you really Santa Claus?"

With time grizzling my beard and adding extra padding to my belly, even I'll admit that I now look an awful lot like Santa, even in plain clothes. So I get this question *a lot,* everywhere I go. I may have made some fumbles in my early years as Santa, but after two decades of fielding questions from inquisitive children, some trial and error, and a whole lot of Christmas inspiration, I know how to answer this one. Whenever a child asks me this question, I'll bend down so I'm at their eye level, give a wink, and whisper the truth: "Well, now . . . that's for you to decide."

FOUR

Do You Believe?

O VER THE NEXT FEW CHRISTMAS SEASONS, my phone started ringing earlier and earlier in the year with requests for home visits. I was delighted! It became such fun, especially now that I'd perfected my private Santa appearances, right down to answering where my reindeer were parked and making a graceful exit once the kids were happily absorbed in unwrapping their toys.

One morning in early November, I received a call from a woman who began the conversation in an unusual way: "I understand you're a naturally bearded Santa," she said.

"Why, yes, I am a naturally bearded Santa," I responded proudly.

The woman continued, "My son is starting to not believe in Santa. We've had a few Santas come over to our house in the past, but they've always had fake beards. This year, he told me he's noticed the fake beards all along, and he doesn't think Santa exists. So I'm looking for someone with a real beard. I heard that you're quite good with children and that you make a very believable Santa Claus."

It happens to every child at some point. Maybe an older sibling who has outgrown Santa or a too-big-for-their-britches classmate bursts their bubble. Sometimes the Christmas season doesn't pan out as they'd hoped and they grow skeptical. Or maybe, like Kevin, they see a bit of unwelcome reality peeking out from under the magic and they're not quite sure what or who to believe. Their little hearts are torn as they start to wonder, "Does Santa Claus really exist?"

I wasn't quite sure how I would convince Kevin that it was still worth it to believe in Santa Claus, but I knew I had to try. No matter their age, I believe that all children deep down *want* to believe; sometimes they just need a little help.

"I'd be happy to come there," I told Kevin's mother. "When would you like me to visit?"

"How about the week before Christmas. Are you available then?"

"I have a few openings left, yes. But let me make a suggestion, if you wouldn't mind. If possible, I'd like you to put together some information about what's go-ing on in Kevin's life at the moment. The more Santa knows, the more real I'll seem to him."

I'd started to do this frequently with home visits, ever since I saw how revealing that little detail of know-ing the kids' 8:30 bedtime had made such a difference my first time out. Whenever there was time, I'd ask parents to put together some notes that I could review about what their children had done recently: good grades on tests, accomplishments in sports, or even things they might have gotten in trouble for during the past few weeks . . . anything to make Santa seem like he knew all about them.

With two weeks before the visit, Kevin's mother had ample time to load me up with all sorts of details. I knew Kevin's little brother was Patrick. I knew the names of all his grandparents, plus the names of his teacher, school principal, and Little League coach. I knew he misbehaved the week before at Chuck E. Cheese's. I even knew that he had lost a tooth recently and how much the Tooth Fairy had left for him. I was ready.

A few days before Christmas, I drove to a friendly little house in a nearby town. Seeing that Kevin's par-ents had left the toys for him outside in a bag, I picked up the bag, walked to the front door, jingled some bells that I now carried with me, and gave a jolly "Ho, ho, ho!"

Kevin's mother opened the door and said, "Look who's here!" I saw Kevin sitting in his pajamas in the living room watching television. As soon as he heard his mother, he turned toward me.

"Santa!" he exclaimed. For a split second, he got that familiar look of awe and excitement—and then he froze. I could see the internal struggle on his freckled face. Half excited, half skeptical, Kevin eyed me warily as I went in and sat down on the sofa next to him.

"Hi, Kevin," I said warmly. I usually brought along some candy canes to hand out to children, so I gave him one.

"Thanks," Kevin said tentatively as he took it.

"You know, Kevin, Mrs. Claus is friends with the Tooth Fairy, and they both tell me to remind kids to make sure they brush their teeth. That way, the Tooth Fairy won't have to give you another fifty cents for a while like she did right after Thanksgiving." Kevin looked surprised. How did Santa know how much the Tooth Fairy had given him, and when?

Kevin wasn't ready to let down his guard quite so easily. "Are you the real Santa?" he asked me abruptly, a serious expression on his young face.

"Well, what do you think?" I asked.

"We've had other Santas come to visit. But they weren't the real one. I could tell because they had fake beards."

"You know, Kevin," I said, smiling, "Santa Claus can't be everywhere. So I have helpers who keep an eye out when I can't. I also listen to what moms and dads tell me about how their children have been behaving. Your teacher, Mrs. Harris, will tell me if kids have acted up in class. Your principal, Mr. Patterson, tells me anytime a student is sent to his office. Even your Little League coach told me that you're really enthusiastic and he's proud of how well you play, but you really need to choke up on the bat when you swing." Of course, Kevin's coach had been telling him the very same thing, and I could see Kevin's eyes open a little wider with each nugget of information Santa seemed to know about him.

I saw Kevin looking intently at my beard, silently searching for a strap or glue. "You're wondering if my beard is real, huh?" Kevin nodded. "Well go on and give it a little tug."

Very cautiously, Kevin reached up and lightly touched my beard. I said, "Oh, it's okay. You can give it a proper tug." And so Kevin pulled my beard, and I gave out a loud "Oop!"

He immediately let go of my beard, and I said, "Ho, ho, ho! I'm just kidding around, Kevin! It didn't hurt at all. As a matter of fact, that's what helps it grow."

I could see the lingering doubt on Kevin's face, and I knew I hadn't completely convinced him that Santa was real. And then that magical, reliable Christmas inspiration kicked in. I put my hand on the boy's shoulder and said, "You know, Kevin, it's okay to stop believing in Santa."

He looked shocked to hear me say this. "It is?"

"Oh, sure," I said reassuringly. "You see, Santa only visits children who believe in him. There comes an age where children start telling each other that there is no Santa Claus, and they stop believing. And that's okay, because there are a lot of other children being born, and it gives me an opportunity to take care of them. Of course, when children stop believing in me, parents usually take over the job of getting the presents. But parents tend to be very practical about their gifts, so they start giving kids things like socks and underwear for Christmas."

When he heard this last piece of information, Kevin's face went from dubious to panic-stricken, and he shouted loudly, "Oh, I still believe!"

Over the following years, I would use the "as older kids stop believing in Santa, new ones are just starting to believe" concept with countless children who had begun to doubt the existence of Santa Claus. I'll do everything I can to keep the magic and mystery of Santa alive for them.

Children want and need to believe that wishes can come true; that's part of the joy of childhood. Santa brings them hope. It's empowering for them to think that there's a system that rewards them for being good, that they have some ability to make their desires come to fruition. Otherwise it's just their parents calling the shots, and parents have to say no all too often. Santa never says no. He just shows up with sparkles and smiles, larger than life, and says, "Maybe, if you're good . . ." That's pretty motivating stuff when you're little!

By the way, it's pretty important to parents for their kids to believe, too. Most parents don't want to see their children grow up too fast and leave behind that sense of wonder. Besides, what better tool is there for motivating good behavior than reminding their kids to be good because Santa is always watching?

I love hearing stories from parents about the lengths they'll go to in order to preserve their children's belief in Santa. They'll stay up until the wee hours on Christmas Eve assembling complicated bicycles, dollhouses, and electronic games so their children never guess the toys didn't arrive fully assembled, via chimney express. Some parents go up into the attic or onto the roof to tromp around, making Santa-like noises. One family even told me they collect dog poop and place it on the lawn on Christmas Eve so their kids will think the reindeer were out there doing their business!

To me, the longer a child believes in Santa Claus, the longer they hold on to their innocence, which is a very precious thing. The world these days is moving at the speed of light, and kids are forced to grow up faster than ever before. Children are exposed to so much, so soon (many six-year-olds I've met are more technologically savvy than their parents!), and they have challenging and complex problems at a much earlier age. Theirs is a complicated world, but Santa is simple. He doesn't pressure them to do well on tests, or lecture them about table manners, or concern them with the scary stuff out there. Santa is the antidote to all of the stress on their little minds. He is pure love and happiness—a kind, smiling figure who delivers miracles wrapped in glittering tinsel, sprinkled with wonder. He lets kids stay kids just a little bit longer.

And isn't that what we all wish for our children?

❄

THE MAGIC OF BELIEVING DOESN'T JUST HAPpen for children. It can happen to adults, as well—and sometimes even to me.

I was sitting in an airport terminal in Syracuse, New York, one day, on my way home from a meeting as part of my non-Santa job. I had a rare few minutes to myself, so I opened up a newspaper and settled in to read a bit. I wasn't halfway through the first page when I heard a squeaky little voice coming from the other side of the pages. "Hi, Santa!"

Putting down the paper, I saw a little blonde cutie-pie, perhaps six or seven years old, with curly hair and two blue eyes fixed squarely on me. She didn't seem at all nervous or even hesitant.

I smiled at her and said, "Hello there."

"It's me, Katie. Do you remember me?"

I'd never seen this little girl before in my life, but I knew she believed she was in the presence of Santa Claus, and I didn't want to disappoint her. "Oh, sure, Katie. How are you doing?"

"I've been really good this year!" she said confidently.

"Oh, that's great," I said.

Katie continued, "My sister Julia is going to come over here and tell you that she's been good, too, but she hasn't been as good as me. And you see baby Tabitha over there?" She pointed to an infant being cradled by a woman sitting nearby. "Since Mama brought Tabitha home from the hospital, she hasn't done anything but poop and cry, so she doesn't deserve anything this year!"

I'd learned by then to expect the unexpected from children, but sometimes one would say something that made it hard not to burst into laughter. Fortunately, being Santa Claus comes with a built-in way of handling such situations. "Ho, ho, ho!" I chuckled merrily.

Then Katie's sister Julia sauntered over to join the conversation. "Hi, Santa," she said, as if she'd just walked into her living room at home and seen a familiar friend. And just as Katie predicted, she, too, announced that she'd been good all year.

"But not as good as me!" Katie made sure to say.

I gave out another "Ho, ho, ho!" and added, "Look, I know you're both trying to be as good as you can be. But do you wanna do Santa a favor to make sure you have a really *great* Christmas?"

They both perked up and said, "Sure!"

"Well," I continued in a lowered voice, leaning in close to them, "I'm guessing that ever since Mama brought home little Tabitha from the hospital, she's had to pay a lot of attention to her. And your mom is probably pretty tired. So what I want you girls to do is to be especially good and help out around the house. You know, like pick up your dishes and bring them into the kitchen, keep your rooms clean, and make sure that you don't get on your mother's nerves."

"Okay," they said in unison.

"So, girls." I looked at them both in the eye. "Do you think your mom wants you two wandering away from her in a busy airport?"

"Probably not," Katie said.

"Well, I think it's time you went back to your mom and waited with her until your plane takes off. Okay?"

"Okay, Santa," they both said. "Bye-bye."

I waved and then went to pick up my newspaper to continue reading it.

"That was so cute!" The voice came from a middle-aged woman sitting across from me.

I looked at her and smiled. "That's what I do."

"It's almost like you're the real Santa," she mused.

"Maybe I am," I said with a wink, and went back to my newspaper.

A few minutes later, the airline began boarding our flight. I stood in the line slightly ahead of the middle-aged woman. Back then, photo IDs were checked at the gate before boarding. So I handed the flight attendant my driver's license, she looked at it and passed it back to me, and I started walking toward the Jetway. Then I heard that same woman behind me ask the flight attendant, "What was the name on his ID?"

I paused a moment, leaning back to hear the answer.

"Santa Claus," she replied matter-of-factly. I glanced over at the attendant, and as the woman walked past her, the attendant turned to me and gave me a thumbs-up and a big grin.

My seat was on the aisle in row 3. So most of the rest of the passengers—perhaps a hundred or so—had to walk past me on their way to their seats. Some of them did little double takes as they went by. I've always found this interesting, how adults act around me. It's so funny that even when I'm not in costume, they'll react.

As the aircraft started to taxi away from the gate, the pilot's voice came over the speaker, telling us the flight duration and weather conditions. And then he said, "I'm told we have a famous celebrity on board with us today, and I'd like to extend a special welcome to him."

My ears perked up, as I wondered what famous person might be flying from the middle of upstate New York. The captain continued, "You may have recognized him as you walked onto the plane. So everyone should try to be good, because I'm sure he's making his list."

And then I realized the pilot was talking about me. I assumed that the flight attendant had told the cockpit crew what happened at the gate, and I smiled to myself.

A short while later, after the plane took off and beverages had been served, the flight attendant who had checked my ID at the gate walked over to my seat.

"Here," she said, handing me a stack of napkins with a mischievous smile. "These are for you."

"What are these?" I asked.

"Letters to Santa," she beamed. "Some of the passengers wrote their Christmas wishes down on their napkins and asked me to give them to you. Then some others overheard and wanted to do it, too. Pens got passed around, and I promised everyone I would make sure you got them all."

From my earliest days handing out charity presents for the toy drive in South Carolina, people would give me letters that children had written to Santa Claus. Sometimes the parents would give them to me, and I imagine they never really thought about what happened to the letters after they handed them over. In fact, they probably assumed I just threw them away. But I never did—and I still don't. They contain children's innermost wishes, and I could never bring myself to simply toss their letters aside or throw them in the trash. So I've read each and every letter to Santa that I've ever been given.

But as I sat there on the plane, I breathed in this surreal moment of getting handed letters to Santa written entirely by adults. I put on my reading glasses and looked at this stack of napkins with scribbled notes on them. What would grown-ups ask Santa for?

Of course, many people wanted a winning lottery ticket, trips to Hawaii, that sort of thing. One man wrote, "My wife is starting a small business, and she'd really appreciate it if you could bring her a new copy machine."

Some of the letters made me laugh. One of them said, "Don't want much. A yacht and my own private island would be just fine."

And then there were a few that touched my heart. One said, "Santa, my son is fighting in Afghanistan. Please bring him back home safely to me." Another woman asked that she and her husband be blessed with a child. There were quite a few that asked for a family member to get well, or to find their soul mate, or for peace on earth. I read every letter. I would likely never get to know anyone who was on that plane personally— or even learn their names—but for one special moment, I shared something truly wonderful with all those people.

Did these adults actually believe I was Santa Claus? Well, who can really say? But I don't think that's what this was all about. I've never been able to explain the phenomenon of adults loving Santa, but I have a theory that seeing me jogs happy memories. I think a lot of us wish we could be children again, becoming breathless with Christmas excitement and believing with all our hearts that wishes can come true. I know I do! I think every grown-up wants to recapture that sense of wonder, even for a moment. And that's exactly what Santa Claus allows them to do.

❄

YOU'RE NEVER TOO OLD TO EXPERIENCE CHRIST-mas magic.

There are those among us who might think that perhaps their time for believing in fairy tales such as Santa is behind them. That is, until a spark of Christmas enchantment brings up all the warmth and cheer of a special holiday memory from long ago.

A grandmother once asked me to come to her home to do for her grandson Joshua what I'd done for Kevin: restore his belief in Santa. Joshua's older brother had reached the age where he and his friends started saying that Santa Claus wasn't real, and Joshua began believing it, too. So, much as I did with Kevin, I visited Joshua's home and told him all about how older children stop believing so younger ones could fill their spots, and once he heard that parental gifts like socks and underwear might be the presents under his future Christmas tree, he was back on board. But for some reason, that day, I didn't stop there. Call it what you will—Santa's sixth sense, or a flash of Christmas inspiration—but something else suddenly popped into my mind, and I found myself telling the following story almost before I even realized it.

"You know, Joshua, when your grandmother was your age," and I pointed over at her, "she lived out in the countryside, not in a big city. She started not to believe in Santa, so her dad brought her to a Sears Roebuck store in town where I was talking to children. She sat right here on my left leg and told me that she wanted a Chatty Cathy doll. And that year, because she was so good, I gave her a Chatty Cathy doll, even though she was starting not to believe in me."

The odd thing was that Joshua's grandmother had never told me that story. Indeed, I knew virtually nothing about the woman other than her address and what she'd told me about Joshua. But as I looked over at her, I noticed a tear tracing its way down her cheek.

Joshua's grandfather broke in, "Well, Santa, I know you're busy, and we've got a little Christmas card for you." The Christmas card served as a code word for when my clients were ready to wrap up my visit.

As Joshua's grandmother walked me to the door and handed me my "Christmas card," I noticed her staring intently at my face, seeming to meticulously examine every detail. Then she whispered to me, "When I was a little girl, I told my father that I didn't believe in Santa.

And he took me to a Sears Roebuck store. I did sit on Santa's lap and ask for a Chatty Cathy doll. And I got it that year."

I smiled and said knowingly, "Yes, indeed." Oddly, I wasn't all that surprised. Seems this was just another one of those unexplainable mini-miracles that I've experienced in my life as Santa Claus.

She looked at me with complete seriousness and asked, "Are you the *real* Santa?"

I tipped my head slightly, gave a wink, and said, "I am what I am."

Christmas magic.

FIVE

Even the Smallest Child
Can Make a Difference

AS I CAME TO REALIZE VERY EARLY IN MY days wearing the red suit, children believe in Santa because Santa believes in children. He understands and appreciates their uniqueness, their passion for the things they love, and their special view of the world. Above all else, he treats them with dignity and respect. Santa knows that children have opinions and ideas that matter—and that sometimes they have valuable lessons to teach us.

I feel especially blessed to have seen and experienced life through the eyes of one particular child: my stepdaughter, Ashley. I honestly believe I would not have become such a believable and authentic Santa Claus had she not been there to help shape my understanding of children. They don't call Santa Claus "Father Christmas" for nothing, you know! As she grew up, Ashley never ceased to surprise and amaze me (and indeed, as an adult, she still amazes me to this day). Not only did she continually bring joy into my life, she showed this Santa just how important one child can be in the world.

When Ashley was just five years old, our family participated in a toy drive for a local orphanage. Believing Ashley to be old enough to understand, Linda and I explained to her that not every little boy and girl has as good a life as she did. Not everyone has a nice house, or two loving parents, or even enough money to buy toys.

"Imagine how you'd feel if you didn't have any toys to play with," I told Ashley. "Would that make you sad?" This seemed to be a good opportunity to teach Ashley about being charitable. Little did I know that it would be Ashley who'd be teaching me a thing or two about generosity that Christmas season.

"Yes, it would definitely make me sad," she said somberly.

"Well, then let's think about all the dolls and toys you have in your room that you don't play with anymore. Do you think that a little girl who doesn't have any toys of her own might enjoy playing with them?"

"I guess . . ." Ashley seemed to be having a little trouble with the concept, so Linda and I walked into her bedroom and started looking for toys that she hadn't played with in a long time. We found plenty. Linda fished out from under the bed a brightly colored plastic hippo.

"Hey, Ashley," Linda asked. "Do you ever play with this anymore?"

"No," she scoffed. "That's for babies."

"Well," I suggested, picking up the hippo and pretending to examine it. "Do you think that a baby somewhere with no toys would like to play with this one now that you're done with it? All toys want to be played with, you know."

Ashley still seemed a little confused by this line of logic. So I tried one more approach. "Ashley, what if we pretended that this was a brand-new toy and wrapped it up like a Christmas present? Then we could go out and give it to a baby with no toys and give him or her a Merry Christmas."

Ashley thought about this, and then we saw the light go on in her head. "Yeah! A baby with no toys would love to get this as a present!"

"What about all the other toys you don't want anymore," Linda said, pulling out a stuffed Elmo doll. "Like this one?"

"Uh-huh," Ashley nodded excitedly. "A baby would like that one, too!"

"Well, let's see how many old toys we can find," I said and smiled, adding, "The more we can give away, the more little kids will have Christmas presents this year!"

Ashley jumped into the activity, and within a few

minutes, we'd put more than a dozen of her old, un-wanted toys in the car to take to the donation center. She was clearly getting into the spirit, and my Santa instincts told me there was even more good to be done here.

"Sweetheart," I kneeled down to her eye level. "I bet some of your friends down the street also have old toys that they don't play with any longer."

Ashley grinned. "Oh, yeah. I'm sure they all do!"

"Well," I said, "imagine how many more babies and little kids could get Christmas presents if some of your friends gave away their old toys, too."

A look of wild excitement spread across Ashley's little face. "Can I go over to their houses and see? Can I? Right now?"

"I think that would be a great idea!" I said. "Then just bring those toys back here and put them into the car with the others. I'll leave the trunk open for you."

Ashley tore off down the street. We lived in a safe, quiet neighborhood with little traffic, and the kids would frequently run over to each other's houses for spontaneous play dates. Linda and I figured Ashley would probably get distracted and be gone for a few hours.

Indeed, we didn't see Ashley again until just around lunchtime, when she ran into the house, out of breath, and grabbed me urgently by the sleeve. "Sal! Sal! Come quick! You've got to drive the toys over to the kids *right now*!"

"Slow down, Ashley," I said calmly. "There's no rush. We can go later this afternoon, after we finish lunch."

"No! It has to be right now!" Ashley was emphatic.

"Why?"

"Because there's no more room left in the car!"

I smiled. I imagined they'd filled up the trunk and had a few more toys that wouldn't fit. So I went outside to see if I could do a little rearranging to placate Ashley before we ate lunch. As I approached the car from the back, I saw the trunk overflowing with toys. *Wow*, I thought. *She's been busy!* I'd never be able to close it without moving some toys to the backseat.

"See?" Ashley said. "There's no more room!"

"Oh, there's more room, honey," I said patiently. "We'll just put some of these toys in the backseat."

"But the backseat's full, too!"

I stopped for a second and thought about that statement. With the trunk open, I couldn't see into the rest of the car. Just how many toys had Ashley collected from her friends?! I slowly walked around the car and looked inside.

Toys were everywhere! The backseat was loaded up so high that I couldn't see out the back window, and on the front passenger seat was another huge pile of toys, leaving barely enough room for me to get in and drive. I was speechless.

"There's a few more kids who want to give away

more of their old toys," Ashley reported, all business. "But we need you to drive these there first."

"Ashley," I said, scratching my head, "how in the world did you collect *all* these toys?" I was baffled as to how this little pipsqueak had managed to get so many kids to give away this much stuff.

"Oh, that was easy," she replied matter-of-factly. "I told them all about how other little kids didn't have stuff, and how sad that would be, and that our toys would make them feel happy for Christmas. And then everyone wanted to help!"

At five years old Ashley had done all this. She'd galvanized an entire neighborhood of kids to give in the name of helping others. I couldn't imagine feeling more proud of my daughter, but Ashley wasn't quite finished impressing us yet.

Two years later, Ashley had reached second grade. One day, Linda and I received an unexpected phone call to come into school to meet with her assistant principal. Ashley was an exemplary student who behaved well, excelled in her classes, and was well liked by her teachers and classmates. These kinds of calls from the school usually meant a kid had gotten into big trouble for something, so Linda and I were both surprised and concerned when the assistant principal asked us to schedule an in-person meeting as soon as possible. We came in the very next morning.

"Mr. and Mrs. Lizard," the assistant principal said warmly as he came out of his office to greet us. "Please come in and have a seat." We all sat down, and the assistant principal continued, "First, let me say that Ashley is such a delight. We all enjoy her. She's very bright, does her work, and contributes to the class."

Linda smiled with pride. I, on the other hand, said simply, "But . . . ?"

My wife looked at me with a stern expression. I explained my comment. "There's obviously a 'but' coming, or else we wouldn't be here." I turned to the assistant principal. "So what's going on?"

"Well," the assistant principal's expression turned serious. "Ashley refuses to participate in the rope climb in the gym."

This actually surprised Linda and me. A very athletic little girl, Ashley had never shown any fear of heights or climbing. And this seemed like the sort of activity our daughter would enjoy immensely.

"She's physically able to do it," the assistant principal continued, "but she simply refuses to do it when the teacher tells her to."

"Has anybody asked her why?" I inquired. If I'd learned anything about Ashley, it was that she could set her mind to something like nobody's business. But I also knew she was generally a cooperative little girl, so there had to be more to this story.

"No, we haven't."

"Well, bring her little bottom down here, and let's figure out why she's being so stubborn," I suggested. The assistant principal asked his secretary to go get Ashley.

While we were waiting, the assistant principal said, "I'm sure you can appreciate that we can't really have our students question or challenge teachers when they tell them to do something."

Linda pointed at me. "That's all my husband's fault," she said, as if tipping off the police to the identity of a dangerous criminal. "He teaches her to think for herself."

"That's right!" I declared. That was proud papa talking, but I knew Santa would have wholeheartedly agreed. Naughty: never okay. But self-confident? Absolutely.

"Well," the assistant principal admonished me, "when an adult tells Ashley to do something, she should just do it, no questions asked."

I shook my head resolutely. "No, I don't agree," I said.

The assistant principal looked completely shocked. "What do you mean?"

"If somebody drives up next to Ashley on the street corner and says, 'Get in the car,' I don't want her doing it just because it's an adult telling her to do something. I want her to run away. Telling kids to simply do anything an adult tells them to without questioning it is how children get in harm's way."

"Well," the assistant principal said, "if it's her teachers

telling her to do something, that's not the same as a stranger telling her to do something."

He had a point there, but so did I. "If Ashley's teachers tell her to do something and she doesn't understand why she's being told to do it, I think she deserves an explanation. I think every kid deserves that kind of respect, don't you? Ashley's reasonable. If you explain to her why, she'll be willing to do it."

Just then, we noticed Ashley standing timidly in the office doorway. The assistant principal invited her in and closed the door behind her.

I walked over to our daughter and said, "Ashley, you don't want to climb the rope in gym class?"

"No," she said quietly.

"Why not?" I asked her gently. I put my hand on her shoulder, wordlessly assuring her that it was safe to speak her mind.

"Well, I watched that safety video with you, and it said that if you're working more than six feet off the ground, you have to be wearing a safety harness in case you fall."

The assistant principal looked a little confused, so I explained to him that I worked as an industrial safety consultant and that Ashley would often sit down and watch the training videos with me.

"So, Ashley," I turned back to face her, "that still doesn't explain why you won't climb the rope."

"Well, they want me to climb higher than six feet, and I don't have a safety harness on."

I hadn't realized that Ashley paid any attention to these workplace safety films, let alone that she understood them and remembered so many details. I was reminded of that early lesson I'd learned my first season as Santa Claus: Never underestimate the observational powers of children. They don't miss a thing!

For a brief moment, I felt pretty amazed at my daughter, until my admiration suddenly turned into serious concern. I looked over at the assistant principal. "How high is it that you're expecting her to climb?"

The assistant principal didn't look at all troubled by the question. "Oh, the gymnasium ceiling's only about fifteen feet off the ground."

"And you want them to climb all the way to the top?" I asked.

"If they can, yes."

"So what happens if they fall?"

He stammered, "Well, we have mats—"

I interrupted, "Wait a minute! Are you talking about those thin blue pads? They're only an inch of foam! What's that going to do if a kid falls from fifteen feet up?"

The assistant principal started looking uncomfortable, and I was furious. "I think Ashley is right," I said. "The kids should be in safety harnesses if they're going to climb."

The assistant principal tried to go back on the offensive. "Mr. Lizard, that's not the reason you came in today. We need Ashley to listen to her teachers and climb the rope when she's told to."

"No," I said forcefully. This was ridiculous! "She's not going to be told that because I don't want my daughter to get injured. You know, we all say our children are the most precious things in the world, and all of their teachers in school talk about how these kids are our future. And yet, we're not doing a very good job protecting them here. Even worse, you're not listening to what Ashley is saying—*and she's right!*

"The Occupational Safety and Health Administration requires that grown men who are working more than six feet off the ground either have a guardrail around them or wear a harness in case they fall. And you're mandating that little kids climb even higher with nothing but an inch of foam padding to break their fall? That's preposterous. So, no, Ashley is not climbing that rope unless she's wearing a harness." I finished my rant in a huff of anger.

You can probably imagine the ensuing controversies, budgetary analyses, arguments at parent-teacher meetings, stories in the media, and fund-raising events. But finally, Ashley got her harness. The school installed a special pulley system in the gymnasium, and parents volunteered to hold the other end of the harness as children climbed the rope in gym class.

I'll always remember how proud I felt that my daughter had the courage to stick to her convictions and not do something she felt was wrong. She proved that even a seven-year-old child can be responsible for significant changes in the world. And truths like that lie at the very heart of what Santa Claus believes. Every child is special, every child is important, and every child deserves our respect. No child's opinions or ideas should ever be stifled or ignored.

Because ultimately, as Santa knows, the smallest among us can sometimes make the biggest difference.

SIX

❄

"Santa, Can I Come Back as an Elf?"

FOR THREE YEARS, MY EXPERIENCES BEING
Santa Claus provided countless moments of joy for
me. I honestly could not imagine feeling anything else
while wearing the red suit. Unfortunately, I was about
to discover that being Santa Claus could also break my
heart.

The Christmas season of 1995 started out on a very
positive note. Word of mouth continued to spread about
me, and between new families and return engagements,
I had more than doubled my total number of appoint-
ments from the previous year. I still did not charge for
appearing, requiring only that the family show me a receipt for their children's charity donation. The thought

that I could help make a difference in that way was one of my favorite parts about being Santa Claus.

With that feeling of holiday giving in my heart, I agreed to a special request that year. At the time, Linda worked as a nurse for a children's hospital in Charleston. Her fellow staff members knew that I played Santa Claus during the holiday season, and they asked me to come to the hospital for a day and visit the children.

The hospital folks told me that I would not need to hand out presents. They already had ample toys for the children to play with, and with five floors worth of young patients, it presented too much of a logistical challenge to carry around that many gifts during my rounds. So instead, the nurses would tell the patients that Santa just stopped by to visit and have a quick chat with all the children.

As in many hospitals, different floors specialized in different medical treatments. Some patients had minor illnesses and injuries, but others had more serious conditions that would keep them there through the holidays. The nurses informed me whenever I was about to talk to a child who would not be home for Christmas, and I assured these kids I would bring their presents to the hospital. This alleviated a lot of concerns from children who feared not getting presents for Christmas if they weren't home in their own beds on Christmas Eve.

I had been visiting for a couple of hours when my

nurse guide took me to the burn unit. As a child, I was badly burned when my mother accidentally tripped over me and spilled a pot of boiling water on my shoulder, and I have a scar to this very day. So I felt a special empathy for the pain and discomfort those children in the burn ward had to go through, especially when their dressings needed to be changed and their wounds cleaned. I remembered how intensely painful that part of the healing process had been. But nothing could have prepared me for Timothy.

I visited a few other children in the burn ward first, most with minor injuries and a few bandages in various places. I spoke with all of them, and they appeared generally upbeat and excited about Christmas, despite being in the hospital. They all seemed comforted by the fact that they'd be going home fairly soon.

As the nurse led me to a room at the end of the hallway, she stopped before taking me inside. "This last patient is Timothy," she said in a barely audible whisper, almost choking back tears. "They brought him in with severe burns over most of his body. He's very weak, and the doctors don't expect Timothy to make it until Christmas."

"Oh, my God," I said, choking back some tears of my own.

"We'd understand if you want to skip this room," she tried to sound as supportive as she could. "After all, you didn't volunteer to visit children in critical condition."

"I couldn't do that to him," I said, feeling absolutely committed to going into Timothy's room. "Santa Claus doesn't care how sick a child is, and maybe my visit will help him get better."

"You're a wonderful man," the nurse put her arm on my shoulder and leaned in closely. "There's one very important thing, though." She looked over her shoulder to make certain Timothy's hospital room door was closed. "Timothy doesn't know how bad his condition is, and his parents don't want him to know. So please act like he'll be getting better and leaving the hospital soon."

I didn't like lying to any child, but I respected the wishes of Timothy's parents. "All right, I understand." I got myself ready as the nurse knocked on the door.

"Timothy?" she said quietly as she pushed open the door a little. "Are you awake? You have a special visitor."

"Who is it?" I heard a small, weak voice ask from inside the room.

"Well," said the nurse with a warm smile, "why don't I let him introduce himself?" She opened the door wide and motioned me to come in.

Usually I enter a room with a hearty "Ho, ho, ho!" But this time, I walked in softly and came right over to Timothy's bed. "Hello, Timothy. Do you know who I am?"

"You're Santa Claus," he said, smiling. Bandages covered all the parts of Timothy that I could see other than his head. Fortunately, Timothy's face seemed undamaged, and I could see that he was a handsome boy. From the nurse's description, I had imagined Timothy looking much worse. But his smile and bright eyes made me believe for at least one hopeful moment that the doctors were all wrong and that this little boy would be just fine.

"I'll leave you two alone," said the nurse. "Santa, you just come and get me if you or Timothy need anything."

I sat down next to the bed. "So, Timothy, how old are you?"

"I'm eight," he said, still sounding weak. I noticed all the machines around his room, the IV drip, and a balloon in the corner that read "Get Well Soon" tied to a chair.

I chose my next words carefully: "Is there anything special that you'd like to tell Santa?"

Timothy didn't respond. I waited for a few seconds, noticing him looking out the window and realizing that he might be trying to think of what to say. It took a while for Timothy to turn back in my direction, and still he appeared to be hesitant to say anything.

I was about to say something to break the silence when, finally, Timothy looked into my eyes with a very serious expression on his face. "Santa, I have something important to ask you," he said quietly.

"Sure, Timothy. Ask me anything you want to."

"I know that I'm going to die—"

I interrupted him immediately with a smile. "Now, who told you that?"

"I know," he said with a composure far beyond his eight short years. "I hear the doctors and my mom and dad talking when they think I'm asleep. And it's okay. I know the fire was bad, and I got really hurt. I know I'm gonna die very soon . . ."

I started to disagree, but something in his eyes stopped me.

"They say that when you die, you become an angel, right?" He waited for me to answer.

I paused for a second, closed my eyes, and took a deep breath. "Yes, Timothy, a lot of people believe that."

"Well, I don't want to come back as an angel, Santa. I know that being an angel is supposed to be nice and stuff, but what I really want is to come back as an elf and make toys with you at the North Pole. Santa, can I come back as an elf?"

I froze. I didn't know how to respond to Timothy's request. So many things raced through my mind. I didn't want to contradict or interfere with any religious beliefs that Timothy's parents had taught him. And of course, how could I possibly promise to make him a mythical elf?

I found myself turning to stare out the window and think, just as Timothy had done moments before. I could feel Timothy watching me with such hope and expectation on his innocent little face. I had to tell him *something*. As the seconds ticked by, I decided to stall him until I could talk to his parents or maybe some of the nurses to see how they thought I should answer his request.

"Well, Timothy, I'll have to check with my boss . . ." I looked up and pointed at the ceiling. "He's the one who makes these kinds of decisions. But I'll come back and let you know what He says."

"Okay, thanks," Timothy said, smiling. We continued talking for a few more minutes, and then the nurse came back to get me. I told her to make sure to bring me back to see Timothy before I left in the afternoon. *Hopefully by then,* I thought, *I'll come up with a way to answer his question.*

The nurse led me to other floors and many, many more children. I had visited maybe three-quarters of the patients, having been passed along from nurse to nurse with each new floor I visited, when the nurse from the burn ward walked up to me. Seeing her grim expression, I felt a knot in my stomach even before she told me the news. "I know you wanted to visit Timothy once more before you left, but he just passed away."

I started to weep, right there in the middle of the hallway. A small voice in my head told me to hold it together, that it was inappropriate for Santa Claus to be seen crying. The nurse seemed to instinctively know what I needed. "Here," she said, putting her arm around my shoulder and leading me down the hallway, "there's a room where you can be alone for a little while."

I honestly don't recall whether she led me to a hospital room, a break room, a chapel, or a broom closet. All I remember was the nurse closing the door and then falling to my knees. Tears rolled down my face for a few minutes as I prayed for Timothy—that he find the peace that he so truly deserved. And I prayed for myself, for strength enough to make it through the rest of my time at the hospital without breaking down crying.

As I visited the remaining children, I did manage to hold it together. But all I could think of in the back of my mind was how I *should* have answered Timothy's question: "Yes, when you die, that's what will happen because you want it to happen." It would have helped him in his final minutes. But I simply couldn't think of that answer in time.

After Timothy, I made a vow to myself that I would never again leave a child waiting for an answer to a question for Santa. No matter what a child asked me, I would always answer it immediately. And I would never disappoint a child who was suffering. But this tragedy also helped me discover my limits. I decided that I could not visit hospitals ever again. I simply did not have the strength in my heart.

That is, until a second chance came my way many years later, when I had my own healing Christmas miracle. . . .

❄

IN 2010, NEARLY FIFTEEN YEARS AFTER MY experience with Timothy, I got a call from a good friend who was a fellow Santa Claus asking me a favor. By that time, my family and I had relocated to New England, and I'd become a seasoned Santa Claus with much more experience under my shiny black belt.

Professional Santas always do whatever they can to help each other out, so when my friend asked me if I was doing anything during the daytime from December 6 to December 10 that year, I didn't hesitate to say, "Not yet. What do you need?"

"Well, I have an appearance scheduled at a cancer treatment center in Boston, but I just got this incredible offer to play Santa Claus in Japan, and it's just too good of an opportunity to pass up. So I'm trying to find someone to fill in at the hospital for me, and I'd really like for it to be you."

My stomach tightened and my heart leapt into my throat. My thoughts raced back to Timothy. I seldom talked about that incident, but it had locked itself into my memory. In all the years since, I'd never approached a hospital to offer my services. My heart just couldn't bear the sadness and pain of seeing children who might not make it until their next birthday, or even a couple of weeks until Christmas. And I had never quite forgiven myself for falling apart that day and not helping Timothy the way I believed I should have. I'd since learned that there were properly trained Santas who specialized in hospital and hospice visits. Those men have my absolute respect and admiration, and I knew it was best if I left such visits in their capable hands.

Of course, my friend had no idea about what had happened to me previously. So I'm certain he was surprised when I responded, "Actually, I'd prefer that you asked someone else."

"I'll be honest with you, Sal," he began in a serious but sympathetic tone. I don't know whether he suspected that I might be squeamish around hospitals or if he just wanted to sound encouraging. "I'd really hoped it would be you and not someone else, because you're one of the best Santas I know, and you're so believable. These are kids with cancer, and I wouldn't feel right turning this over to someone I didn't trust to make his appearance special for them."

I closed my eyes, and asked myself, *Can I do this?* Could I get through all those gut-wrenching visits, hospital room after hospital room, sick child after sick child, and still be the Santa Claus these children needed me to be? I honestly wasn't certain.

And then I remembered the vow I'd made to myself

the day Timothy died to never disappoint a child who was suffering. Those kids were suffering, to one degree or another, and my fears and limitations seemed very small in comparison. This wasn't about me; it was about delivering sunshine to kids who needed Santa's loving reassurance. I took a deep breath and mustered my strength to sound as confident and committed as I could. "All right, I'll do it."

"Thanks, Sal. This will really mean a lot to those kids," he said, not realizing how much his statement applied to me as well.

My friend provided me with the contact information for the director of the cancer treatment center, a woman named Lisa, who called me the following day. Lisa explained to me that her facility, a clinic attached to a much larger hospital, specialized in outpatient cancer treatment for children ranging in age from newborns to teenagers. Each year, the clinic would put on a special series of events to entertain their young patients at Christmastime. Santa Claus, of course, played an essential part in the program, along with jugglers, a cartoon artist, and more. Starting the following Monday through Friday, I would work from 10:00 A.M. to 1:00 P.M., visiting with the kids and handing out presents.

As uplifting as the festivities sounded, I still tossed and turned in bed on Sunday evening, trying to fall asleep while dreading the next five days of my life. *What have I gotten myself into? How am I going to get through this?* Linda tried to ease my mind, assuring me that I'd come a long way since visiting Timothy and that my experience would carry me through, but my heart was still heavy. I don't remember falling asleep, but I definitely remember waking up feeling panicked about the day ahead.

I arrived at the clinic carrying my red suit in a garment bag over my shoulder and found Lisa's office. I knocked on the already-open door, sticking my head inside. "Lisa?" I said to the slender, dark-haired woman sitting behind her desk.

She looked up from her computer and, seeing a white-bearded, portly gentleman standing in her doorway, her face brightened as she said, "Santa! I'm so glad you could make it!"

"Happy to be here," I said merrily, hoping I sounded convincing.

Lisa led me out of her office and down a surprisingly cheerful hallway, decorated with bright furniture and vintage Disney paintings. "Right in here, Santa," Lisa said, opening a door for me. "This is usually a file storage room, and some doctors and nurses use it to fill out paperwork or take a quick break. I'm afraid it's a little full at the moment . . ."

I looked around and saw immediately what Lisa meant. Brightly wrapped presents and toys filled the room almost from floor to ceiling in some places. Stuffed stockings had labels taped to them specifying age ranges like INFANT, TODDLER, 5–8 YEARS, 13 AND OLDER, and so on. I couldn't believe how many toys and presents they had. These folks certainly took their Christmas event seriously.

Fortunately, I also saw a few chairs and tables to put my things down and space to get ready. Lisa backed out into the hallway, saying, "This door doesn't lock, but if it's closed, someone will always knock before walking in. As soon as you're ready, just come back to my office and I'll show you where to go next."

"Great," I said. "Thanks so much."

"Thank *you*, Santa," Lisa said with a grin as she closed the door.

The familiar ritual of putting on my Santa Claus attire steadied my nerves a bit. When I was all ready, I paused and took a deep, calming breath. *Okay, Sal . . . you can do this.*

I walked back into Lisa's office. She gave a gasp and a huge smile. "Oh, the children are going to be so excited! Come on!" She hurried me down the hallway in the other direction, and we entered a huge waiting room filled with children and their families.

I'd never seen a waiting area like this before. It looked more like a kindergarten classroom, filled with toys, books, huge blocks, and even a small slide that younger children could play on. In the center sat a gigantic aquarium filled with brightly colored tropical

fish and elaborate coral formations. Hanging everywhere were festive Christmas decorations.

On one side of the room, I saw an artist doing carica-
ture sketches of some of the children. On the other side,
a brightly dressed juggler entertained the crowd with
jokes and fancy tossing tricks. Against the far wall,
placed in front of a large cardboard cutout of a fairy-
tale castle, I saw a cushioned chair with several stockings placed on either side of it. And next to those
stockings—in bright red dresses with white fur on the
sleeves, collar, and hemline—were two of the loveliest
"Santa's helpers" I had ever seen.

"Over here, Santa," Lisa said, leading me toward the
chair.

Upon hearing the word *Santa*, almost every child
suddenly stopped whatever he or she was doing and began jumping up and down and shouting my name. I
had to smile, even though I felt a little guilty because
the poor cartoonist and juggler had found themselves
quickly abandoned and forgotten as the children began
to spontaneously form a line leading to Santa's chair.

"Santa," Lisa turned to face the two attractive young
helpers, "this is Dr. Kelly and Dr. Stockton."

"You're *doctors*?" I felt suddenly embarrassed by my
surprised reaction. It wasn't their gender so much as
how young they both looked. On the other hand, at the
age of almost fifty-five, more and more folks had started

looking young to me. Nevertheless, I tried to hide my little faux pas by adding, "Aren't you supposed to be wearing white coats?"

The two doctors smiled. "This is our uniform for the week," one of them said.

"And the male doctors are all dressed as elves!" the other one added.

"Okay, Santa," Lisa said, as a young fellow wearing normal clothes and holding an elaborate camera walked up to join us. "This is Paul, our photographer, and he'll take the pictures that we'll give to the parents. Each child will come up and sit on your lap for a minute or two. Then Dr. Kelly will pass you a toy, and Dr. Stockton will hand you a candy cane to give each one. Sound good?"

"Just perfect," I said. As I looked at the line of excited children, I had almost forgotten that we were all in a cancer treatment center.

The first few children all went very smoothly. It felt just like being at a mall. They would sit on my lap, we'd talk for a brief time, Paul would take a few pictures, and then the next child would hop up.

But then I saw a little girl with a tube inserted into her nose, snaking back behind her ear, and then down her chest. She seemed too weak to climb up onto my lap herself, so I reached out for her incredibly carefully so as not to knock out the tube and gently brought her up onto my knee. Everything seemed okay, and I made certain to put her back down just as carefully when we finished.

I didn't want to inadvertently do something wrong and cause one of the children harm, so before the next child came forward, I quickly turned to one of the doctors. "Is there any special way I should be picking them up when they have tubes?" I asked quietly.

"Exactly the way you just did it," she answered.

"Well, that's a relief," I said. "I had no idea how to do it."

"Really?" she looked surprised. "You did that so naturally, I just figured you'd done it lots of times before."

As the line moved on, I realized that not all of these children were patients. Families traveled to the clinic together, with brothers and sisters joining their siblings, and many of the healthier children had gotten into line first. But slowly and steadily, I began to notice more sick and weakened children—their skin a paler color, tubes in noses or arms, a lack of hair on many of their heads, and even a number of children in wheelchairs, too weak to stand up.

All my hesitations vanished as my Santa Claus persona took over completely. I refused to see these children as anything other than children—not sick children or weak children, but just children who each wanted or needed to see a jolly Santa. And so I pushed aside my fears and simply put myself fully at ease with each and every one of them. In turn, they all seemed to be totally comfortable with me.

By the time we got further down the line, some of the children appeared too weak to be lifted out of their wheelchairs. For those kids, I just kneeled down next to them and talked at eye level, allowing Paul to take some wonderful photos.

Some children felt embarrassed to have their picture taken because they had lost their hair. I would never force a photo on any child, but a few parents of some of the more reluctant children asked me if I could maybe convince their son or daughter to take a picture anyway. And so I would try a number of different approaches. In one case, I posed with my chin on top of a boy's head, my beard completely covering up his baldness, which made him giggle.

Another girl who looked to be around ten years old told me that she felt ugly without her hair. I responded in a soft and gentle voice, "You know, you don't need hair to look beautiful," and I took her chin and lifted it up to look directly into her pretty eyes. "I can see that you're a very beautiful little girl. I bet your parents think so, too, right? They'd love to get a photo of you with Santa. And I'll be honest with you: it would be a true honor for me to have a picture taken with such a beautiful little girl."

She smiled for the photo—a sincere and touching

smile from the heart—and I caught a glimpse of her parents, off to the side, crying when they saw a joyful look on their precious daughter's face as she sat next to Santa Claus. It was all I could do to keep from shedding a tear myself. None of these children, none of these families, deserved this misfortune. But I held myself together. Santa remained jolly for every child in that waiting area.

After an hour, all the children there had spent their time on Santa's lap, and Lisa came to take Paul and me upstairs to visit with the children who were in private rooms prepping for or recuperating from chemo and radiation. The children on that floor were all lying in beds, so I would sit down next to each one to talk for a while. I kept things light and happy without forcing cheer on anyone. I had learned early on that day not to ask these children what they wanted for Christmas. Most said, "I just want to get better," and as much as I wished I could magically heal each and every one of those kids, that was a gift that was beyond Santa's power to deliver. I would simply answer, "I hope so, too. I really do."

Many of the kids, remarkably, seemed to be in good spirits. One young teenager named Randy, however, had a huge chip on his shoulder—and with good reason. The chemotherapy treatments had left him weak, bald, and pale with dark shadows under his eyes, and he was generally miserable and angry. He scoffed bitterly at the idea of taking a picture with Santa.

Randy's father took me aside. "Santa," he whispered, "this is really important to us. Can you please try to get him to take just one picture with you?"

I looked into this man's eyes and saw a world of anguish, and I knew I had to try. I glanced around the room and spotted my two lovely Santa's helpers.

"Those gals are really cute, aren't they?" I said, pointing to them.

Randy nodded.

"And I'm sure you'd rather have a picture with the two of them, maybe one on each side with their arms around you? That might be fun to show your friends, don't you think?" I looked at the attractive young doctors, who had been watching the whole time, and they nodded with big smiles.

"Yeah, it would . . . ," Randy said, showing just the hint of a smile.

"Well then, here's the deal. You've gotta get through me first. One picture with Santa with a full smile from you, and then I send over my two helpers. You get to keep the picture with them, and your parents get the one with you and me. Deal?"

"Deal," Randy said, his smile widening. I posed for a picture with him grinning, and then my two helpers posed for a photo that I'm sure made Randy the envy of all his friends.

On the way out, Randy's parents stopped me, both with tears in their eyes. "We don't know how to thank you. This will probably be Randy's last Christmas, and we just wanted one more picture of him looking happy. You don't know how much this means to us."

I smiled and quickly turned away to take off my glasses and wipe away my own tears. By then we were done making the rounds upstairs, and Lisa brought me back down to where we'd started. I returned to the filing room to change, and as soon as the door closed behind me, I started sobbing. I just couldn't help it. These poor children—many of them acting so brave, all of them much too young for anything like this. It's unfair enough when an adult has to suffer through cancer, but for a child, it's unthinkable. I managed to compose myself and said good-bye to Lisa on my way out.

The next day, I returned to a similar routine. And again, at the end of the day, I went back to the filing room and shed the tears I'd been holding in check the past three hours. I heard a knock on the door and quickly dried my cheeks.

"Come in," I called.

Lisa walked in and shut the door behind her. She sat down on one of the chairs and pulled out a few tissues from a box on the table next to her. "I hope you'll excuse me," she said, dabbing at her eyes. "But this is the room I come to when I need to cry."

"Oh, then I'm not the only one . . ."

"What do you mean?" she asked.

"I'll be honest with you, Lisa. I was afraid to come

and do this hospital stuff. I was so scared that I might choke up in front of the children. It's hard not to."

"Don't worry," she said reassuringly as she quietly blew her nose. "All of us cry at some point, because we care so much. We wouldn't be in this job in the first place if we didn't care. We just don't cry in front of the patients. We each have our own little space—a filing room, a broom closet, a bathroom stall—where we go to just let it out."

I hadn't ever thought about that. I had been so caught up in my own fear of facing these kids for just five days. But these people went through this *every single day*. "Well, then I don't feel so weird for wanting to cry so much," I said.

"Oh, no! You're not weird at all. It would be weird if you *didn't* cry!"

And somehow, in that one moment, everything changed for me. Call it a catharsis, or whatever you will, but Lisa's words suddenly made everything I felt seem okay. I don't think I will ever stop feeling overwhelming sadness at seeing so many ill children and the pain of their families. But that day, I realized that it's all right to feel that way, and that letting myself cry when I met a sick child doesn't make me a bad Santa. It makes me a real Santa. I cry because I care.

Some of these children might not have much time left, but they deserve just as good of a visit from Santa as everybody else. I hope that my showing up as Santa can raise their spirits. It is one thing to spread cheer to healthy children through winks, smiles, and candy canes, but an entirely different experience being called upon to deliver joy to children who are truly suffering. If it means easing their pain even for a few minutes, then I am wholeheartedly up for the task.

By Friday afternoon, after I said my good-byes to all of the staff, I headed back to my break room. It seemed so empty now. Nearly all of the donated toys and gifts had been handed out. Just as I was finishing lacing up my shoe, Lisa walked in and sat down at the table across from me.

"So, can we sign you up again for next year?" she asked matter-of-factly.

My first thoughts went to my Santa friend who had asked me to fill in. Professional Santas consider it very bad form to steal a client from a fellow Santa Claus, so I politely let Lisa know that I couldn't do that to my friend.

"Oh, no, I wasn't suggesting that," she said. "We'll still use him for something else. The hospital has tons of work for Santa Clauses. But we'd really like to have you back here again next year."

I didn't hesitate at all. "I'd love to, Lisa. Just call me with the dates and I'll block off my calendar for next season."

Five days earlier, I had been dreading the experience. I'd spent fifteen years avoiding appearances at hospitals, fearing I would mess up again. But I had been given a second chance. I drove home that day with a deep sense of satisfaction and completion. This time, I'd gotten it right.

They say that what we give is what we receive, and after this experience, I finally understood what that adage really meant. I'd been asked to deliver cheer to those who needed it most, and in return, I got something far greater. I'd given from the depth of my being, and as a result, my broken heart had finally healed.

※

I STILL THINK OF LITTLE TIMOTHY, EVEN TO this day. I imagine him, somewhere up there in heaven, happily making toys for children and granting their wishes. And instead of feeling anguish, I'm comforted by the thought that maybe, just maybe, there isn't all that much difference between being an angel and being one of Santa's elves after all.

SEVEN

❄️

What Would Santa Do?

SANTA CLAUS ALWAYS SEEMS TO KNOW THE right way to go.

That's why, as I found myself wearing the red suit more and more in public, I frequently came to ask myself: *What would Santa do?* I was becoming increasingly conscious of wanting to live up to Santa Claus's benevolent, honorable standards. And my days as a mall Santa Claus gave lots of opportunities to check in with the bearded beacon of Christmas wisdom for guidance.

By Christmas of 2000, my family and I had relocated to New Hampshire, where I eventually turned my Santa life from a hobby into a sideline career. I built a festive website so people could find me, printed business cards, and joined some networks of professional Santas that I could turn to for guidance, ideas, and advice (including

one that my genes gave me proud access to: The Amal-
gamated Order of Real Bearded Santas). My Christmas seasons were happily filled with home visits and a
few local store events.

I had also, after doing serious homework about the
world of professional Santas, begun charging a nomi-
nal fee, mostly to cover my costs for gas and supplies,
including a second Santa Claus outfit (you'd be surprised how hot it gets under all that velvet, and Santa
must always show up smelling of nothing other than
candy canes and cookies!) and to ensure I could still
support my family through the holiday seasons while I
took time away from my business. I wish there were
some way I could donate all my time to being Santa for
free, but the reality is that Santa has to eat, too. He and
his family can't live on just cookies and milk!

AS HAPPY AS I WAS IN MY SANTA LIFE, ANOTHER EXCIT-
ing turn was right around the corner. One morning in
late December 2001, my phone rang. It was a gentleman named Mark from a company called Photo Promotions, asking me in a panicked voice if I could get to
a nearby mall within an hour to do an emergency fill-in
for the mall Santa they had hired.

"Sure can!" My voice may have sounded calm, but
my heart was racing with excitement. My first job as a
mall Santa—I'd finally made it to the big time!

Fully dressed in Santa Claus regalia, I raced over to the shopping center and followed the instructions Mark had given me. Apparently, mall Santas don't simply walk in through the main entrance, nor do they cut through Sears or Macy's. Instead, they enter through a special employee service door, unmarked so that mall patrons won't notice it. *That was smart,* I thought. Kids shouldn't see Santa waltzing in the front doors like a regular holiday shopper.

Unfortunately, it being the Saturday before Christmas, the parking lot was jam-packed, and the only spot I could find was far from my special entrance. *This isn't good,* I thought. Kids shouldn't see Santa picking his way through the slush and snow in a mall parking lot, either!

As I headed toward the mall, I saw a family walking through the lot with their kids in tow. *Oh, no!* I ducked down and hid between two cars, crouching until I saw them safely pass by. I took a few more steps toward the mall when I saw another family approaching, and I quickly ducked back down until they were gone. Then another family walked by . . . and another. I probably hid about six or seven times. The whole episode was like some crazy scene from a spy movie, except the spy was a forty-six-year-old bearded fat man dressed in a full Santa Claus outfit.

I finally made it to the unmarked door, where Mark greeted me and led me through what felt like a secret passageway (really, it was a dimly lit corridor between stores, but I was so filled with excitement that everything seemed enchanted). We paused in front of two double doors and he said, "Okay, are you ready?"

I nodded and took a deep breath.

Mark opened the doors into the atrium, and time suddenly stopped for me. I had stepped into a brightly lit mall, glittering from the floor to the rafters with tinsel, ornaments, and other Christmas decorations that adorned every storefront and balcony. Then I spotted the set where Santa would sit. *Oh, my!* Everything radiated outward from a green, velvet-covered, throne-like chair placed next to a fully decorated Christmas tree. Leading up to all of this ornamental splendor, a long red carpet traced its way between two small white picket fences, each covered with large candy cane decorations. I'd finally arrived!

My days as a mall Santa were under way. That first time, I quickly learned the ropes of greeting children, listening as they whispered to me what they wanted for Christmas, and then snapping a picture. At the urging of the Photo Promotions staff, I had to move the long line of holiday patrons along quickly, which I didn't love, but I figured that they knew their business best. Five hours flew by in the blink of an eye. I probably talked to nearly two hundred children, more than I had ever seen in a single day. Some laughed, some cried, but every one had their special moment with Santa. And I felt wonderful.

But as I drove home from the mall, despite the glow from my first day as what I considered a bona fide professional Santa, I had a nagging feeling that something was wrong with the entire setup. The pressure of having to hurry children along through their encounter with Santa didn't seem right to me. Santa Claus's whole world revolved around interacting with children and making them happy, not rushing kids through a line in order to make more money.

There had to be a way, I mused, to be a successful mall Santa and still give children all the attention and love they deserved. How could I make the experience even better for the kids who came to see me? And then I chuckled to myself. I knew exactly where to turn for inspiration.

What would Santa do?

As it happened, I'd have plenty more chances to find out.

❄

THE THREE-YEAR-OLD WHO STOOD NOT THREE feet from my Santa chair was screeching. Not in excitement, mind you—in holy terror. Her mother, likely exhausted from a long day of holiday shopping, tried pleading, cajoling, and finally scolding the child for not cooperating. "We need this for your Christmas card, Ava!" She turned to me and said, defeated, "Just grab her so we can get a picture, okay?"

The Photo Promotions manager nodded and silently motioned for me to do it so we could move the line along. They had a business to run, and I fully appreciated that. But I wasn't in the business of traumatizing kids for the sake of selling a snapshot. The children *must* come first, and Santa Claus would know this.

What would Santa do?

I looked down into the eyes of this frightened little girl, and the answer was right there, plain as day. I could only imagine how intimidating I must have looked to this itty-bitty child, looming from that humongous throne. So I did the unthinkable. I got up out of my Santa chair and sat down on the floor in front of her. Scandalous! A mall Santa does not get out of his chair, except when he heads off to check on the reindeer (in other words, take a break). The photographer was furious, as he had to completely reset his camera and tripod to take a picture of us far below where he had so perfectly framed the shot. But in my heart, I knew Santa wouldn't let something like that stop him. He would do whatever he needed to do in order to comfort a frightened child.

It worked. Ava calmed down and actually giggled, seeing Santa plopped on the floor. Although the managers and photographers weren't too pleased with this stunt, it turned Ava's experience with me into a happy one, and that's what mattered.

Over the years, I've given a lot of thought to what frightens children when they see Santa Claus. Imagine it for a moment from their perspective. Santa, they know, is very powerful. He is the giver of toys. And if you think about it, the most important thing to children, after love, is their toys. He decides whether you've been naughty or nice, and how many toys you'll get as a result. That's a lot of power for one person to have! And no one seems to question his authority.

But the awe and intimidation don't end there. As a young child walking into a large mall, everything about Santa and the elaborate North Pole Village is regal. He sits up on a grand throne, wearing plush velvet with helpers all around him. Meeting Santa, for a child, would feel like meeting a king.

After waiting in a long line for their audience with this important, imposing figure, children find themselves marched unceremoniously up onto a raised platform to meet this "king of toys." The child gets placed, all alone, on the lap of this great icon (who, really, is a total stranger to them), and then is expected to make his or her plea for gifts. I don't know about you, but all this feels a little intimidating even to me—*and I'm the one who plays Santa Claus!*

Understanding and appreciating this made all the

difference for me as a professional Santa, especially when I experienced the one thing that happens to every Santa Claus. That's right: he gets peed on. A child sits down on your lap. You give a hearty "Ho, ho, ho!" and ask if he or she has anything special to tell Santa this year. Suddenly, you feel a warm sensation slowly spread across your upper thigh, and you immediately know what's happened. And so does the child.

Now, the immediate instinct might be to jump up, but I realized early on that a child feels mortified enough already. Imagine: he or she has probably only recently been potty trained, and now here they are disappointing their mom and dad in front of hundreds of strangers. And on the lap of the great and powerful Santa Claus himself, no less!

What would Santa do?

Santa would never, ever blame a child, because Santa understands it's not the child's fault. Santa's been around a long time, and he's seen many, many children. He knows that some of them find meeting him to be a stressful experience. Sometimes I can feel these poor frightened children actually trembling, and often all it takes is a simple "Hello there" from me to push the scared youngsters over the edge, and then they suddenly have an accident.

I would always explain to my helpers that if I gave them a nod while a child was sitting on my lap, it meant they should bring me a small handful of folded up paper towels. I'd inconspicuously blot my thigh and the helpers would immediately turn on the fan to help dry the wet leg. A spritz of fabric freshener would usually hold me over until I could change into my backup suit, which I always have on hand.

Realizing that Santa Claus would put the well-being of a child as his top priority, I always make certain to let the parents know what happened, but without embarrassing the child. After all, most parents have had experience with accidents before and are prepared to deal with them so their child isn't uncomfortable for long. So I wait for Mom or Dad to come over to get their son or daughter, and I'll say to the child, "Let me tell your mom something real quick." Then I quietly inform the parent, "I didn't want to embarrass your child, but I think they just had an accident. It's no big deal, but I thought you should know." The parents I've delivered this news to always seem to appreciate the discretion.

I remember once seeing a long line of children waiting to meet me as Santa, but suddenly no one came up to sit on my lap. I looked over but couldn't quite see what was happening. Finally, one of my helpers walked up to me and said, "Santa, there's a little girl in line named Stacy, and she's very upset."

"Oh, really?" I felt concerned. "Why?"

"Well, she's been waiting a while, and she was getting

ready to come up to see you. But she got so excited, she wet herself. And she thinks you're going to be mad at her."

"Well, you assure Stacy that Santa doesn't get angry at *any* child, and I would love to meet her."

So when she came up, I said, "Hello there, Stacy."

"Hello," she said in a very soft and worried voice.

I didn't want to point out the accident directly. So instead, I got up from my chair, kneeled down next to her, and whispered in her ear, "Your mom wants to get a picture of you with Santa, doesn't she?"

Stacy nodded with a small frown, her lower lip quivering.

I smiled at her and continued whispering, "Stacy, I know you don't want to sit on my lap, but you know what? I'm going to go ahead and stand you up here with me, and I'm going to put my arm around you in such a way that nobody can see that," and I nodded my head toward her wet spot. "And you and I are going to take the best Christmas picture ever. Will that be okay?"

Stacy gave a tiny nod. So as I kneeled down beside her, with our heads at the same level, I put my arm around her waist so that my sleeve draped itself over the wet stain. When Stacy saw what I was doing, I whispered again, "See? Nobody will ever know. It's just our little secret, and now you'll be able to show this photo to all of your friends and family."

Stacy smiled, and we took the picture.

Afterward, Stacy began to walk down off of the raised platform. Then she suddenly turned around, ran back toward me, and flung herself into my arms, squeezing me in a tight hug. With her face pressed next to mine and her mouth next to my ear, she said in a whisper, "Thank you, Santa."

Santa understands . . . accidents happen.

❄

I'VE LEARNED THAT NOW AND THEN SANTA needs to get a little creative in the spirit of keeping Christmas spirits bright.

Malls, as we all know, can be high-stress zones during Christmastime. There are big crowds and lots of hustle and bustle, and of course, long lines . . . especially to see Santa Claus. During the height of the season, some people stand in line for hours waiting to visit with Santa, and my heart always goes out to them. Parents try to keep their squirming little ones entertained, but even the most patient of children can stand up quietly for only so long. Tensions usually run high as people's patience wanes, and I always wished I could do something to extend a little Christmas cheer to these intrepid folks. *Hmmm* . . .

What would Santa do?

One of the rules of being a mall Santa is usually that

Santa Claus can't be in the North Pole Village while he's on his break. It makes sense: when Santa goes on break, so do his helpers. And if Santa stayed on the set, the helpers would need to stay, as well, in order to keep the crowd under control. But I realized this didn't mean that Santa couldn't be out and about *just outside* the North Pole Village, chatting with people in line to keep their spirits up while they waited, now did it?

One year, while I was a Santa-in-residence for the entire Christmas season at a mall in New Hampshire, I decided to give it a try. I took my usual lunch break in the hidden storeroom they kept private for me, but I came out a little earlier than I was expected. I casually wandered over to greet a few of the children in line, hoping no one from the photo company would stop me.

"Are you having a good time at the mall today?" I asked one of the little girls. "That hot dog looks delicious!" I said to another boy.

Before I knew it, I had stopped to have short conversations with scores of different families. A few asked to take their picture with me while they waited, but I gently let them know that I was only supposed to take pictures on the set. Most people accepted that and didn't press the issue.

To my relief, the photo staff seemed perfectly okay with my having these conversations. I suppose, as long as I didn't enter the set itself and didn't leave the mall, they had no problem with a social Santa.

I thought about how frustrated parents and children must feel to be standing in line for forty-five minutes or longer to see Santa, only to be told that Santa would be back in another hour. And of course, parents and their children had to wait around or else they would lose their place in line. So as the days went on, I made it my common practice to eat my lunches and dinners as quickly as I could and then come out to chat with people—both children and adults—always in character as Santa Claus.

But when I looked over at all those people standing farther back in line who could only watch as Santa chatted with other children and parents in line in front of them, I felt guilty. No matter how brief I made my conversations with people, I couldn't get to everyone before my break ended. I imagined how disappointed the children would feel if they were the ones standing too far away from Santa Claus.

Hmmm . . .

If Santa can't make any circumstance merry, then I don't know who can. So I raised my voice a little to get the attention of the few dozen people in my immediate area: "Hey, who here knows the song 'Rudolph the Red-Nosed Reindeer'?" Of course, everybody did. "Would you all like to sing that song with Santa?"

A cacophony of excited children yelling "Yeah!" enveloped me. So I started singing, and I found myself immediately joined by a chorus of children and their parents. As the song went on, the singing got louder and louder. Before I knew it, I could hear many more voices singing than just those few dozen who had started. I looked around and noticed the song spreading up and down the entire line.

By the time the song ended, we must have had hundreds of voices joining in. I didn't want to lose the momentum and enthusiasm of the crowd, so I immediately began singing "Frosty the Snowman," and nearly everyone in line waiting for Santa started singing along again. I could feel the mood of the whole crowd lifting as the songs jollied their stress away.

With an entire line of hundreds of people all singing at the same time, I didn't think the experience could grow any more amazing. But it did. As the line of people in front of me sang "Santa Claus Is Coming to Town," I suddenly heard singing coming from above me, as well. I looked up and saw a few customers starting to come out of the shops and join in, and then even more customers. It seemed, for just a moment, that the entire mall had transformed into one giant Christmas choir.

We sang a few more songs, and then the time came for Santa to get back to work. Everyone applauded each other before returning to the stores and continuing with their shopping. They all seemed to have a little extra spring in their step, buoyed by this collective magical Christmas moment.

So from that day on, I would make certain to eat my

lunch quickly and come out to chat and sing with the crowd. Twice a day, every day, the entire mall would erupt in joyous voices singing, and waiting in line for a photo with Santa didn't seem quite as tedious. As for me, I loved every second of it.

❄

AFTER A FEW YEARS OF BEING A SANTA IN VAR-ious malls, my techniques became rather well-known by many parents. Some even recognized me when they saw me from the line or brought their child up for a picture and would say, "Oh, I'm so glad it's you again! You're really good!"

I'm just doing what Santa would do, I'd think to myself and smile.

EIGHT

Santa's Giggles, Gear, and Gadgets

BEING SANTA CLAUS HAS GOT TO BE THE BEST job in the world. I get to spend two months out of the year hearing children's secret wishes and their pint-size pearls of wisdom. Some of my most treasured memories are the chuckles I've gotten from kids just being open and honest. I never know what they'll say or do next.

I remember once standing in the checkout line at a department store (in non-Santa clothing) when a little girl around four years old came over to me and asked sheepishly, "What's your name?"

I looked over at her mom who was standing a few feet away, and she nodded her approval. So I bent down and replied, "Honey, who do you think I am?"

"I think you're Santa," she said.

"Well," I said and grinned. "Then you'd better be really good."

Her face lit up with pride. "Oh, I am!" she said and smiled broadly. "I'm not even peeing in my underpants right now!"

Yes, kids will say pretty much anything to Santa, much to the embarrassment of many parents I've met. One Christmas season as a mall Santa, I had a little girl of about six sit down and ask me, "Do you ever spank naughty girls?"

I'm sure a look of shock came through in the surprised expression on my face. This was a new one for me. "Absolutely not, sweetie," I said. "Santa would never spank a child. Why, did someone tell you that you needed a spanking?"

She took a big breath the way young children do when they're about to tell you an important story with lots of details. "Well, one time I got up in the night to get a drink of water, and I saw Daddy dressed up like you. He asked Mommy if she'd been naughty or nice, and Mommy said that she'd been naughty. So Daddy said that if she was naughty, then he was going to have to spank her. And then Mommy said she liked when Daddy spanked her."

Oh, boy, I thought, fighting back a smile. I looked up at her parents, who suddenly realized the story their daughter was spilling to Santa. The girl's poor mother was burying her head in her husband's chest, trying to cover her face with her hands. The father, meanwhile, winced and turned bright red.

"Ho, ho, ho!" I said, masking a chuckle. "Sometimes, sweetheart, daddies dress up as Santa, but they don't always get it exactly right. It takes a lot of practice. It sounds like your mommy and daddy were just playing a game. I think the next time you see something like that, you should probably just go back to bed." And with a reassuring smile and a wink, I said in the parents' direction, "And hopefully Mommy and Daddy will learn to play Santa Claus better next year."

At another mall appearance, I had a series of children come up one after the other, each concerned about my weight and health. I learned later that they were all part of the same first grade class and had just finished a unit on nutrition. The first one, a little girl, had two cookies with her. She handed me one and kept the other for herself, saying, "This cookie is for you, Santa. It's sugar-free because I don't want you to get diet Wheaties."

The next child, a little boy, asked me, "Do you ever get stuck in chimneys?"

Then a little girl inquired, "Do you know what your cholesterol level is?"

Finally, a boy looked me up and down and asked me with a straight face, "Santa, did you ever think of giving yourself a gym membership for Christmas?"

But perhaps my most treasured memory didn't make me laugh so much as simply melt my heart. Children usually meander at a normal pace up to my chair to meet me, generally with a parent holding their hand. But one little girl, probably about four years old, came running up to me at full speed in a mall in Massachusetts. Before I could even react, she catapulted up onto my lap, threw her arms around my neck, and started hugging me. So I hugged her back. After half a minute or so, I let go, assuming she would turn around and start talking to Santa, as most kids tended to do.

But she didn't stop hugging me.

I gave her another little hug and let go again. She still continued to hug me, very tightly. By this point, the girl's mother had walked up to the big chair, watching all this with a wide grin on her face. I smiled back and said, rather amusedly, "She's not letting go!"

Her mother continued smiling. "She loves you, Santa. As a matter of fact, when I asked her what she wanted for Christmas, she told me that she just wanted to hug Santa. So I asked her what she wanted Santa to bring her for Christmas, and she said she didn't know. She just wanted to hug Santa. That's all she kept saying; she just wanted to hug Santa."

That left me at a loss for words. After another minute or so, I asked the little girl, "So, is there anything special you want to tell Santa Claus?"

And she kept right on hugging me, without saying anything.

Another minute passed, and I said to her mother in

an apologetic tone, "I don't know how we're going to get the picture."

Without missing a beat, the mother said, "Honey, turn around for the picture." The little girl immediately let go of my neck, spun around on my lap, and leaned against me so the photographer could snap the picture. Then, right after the flash went off, she resumed her determined embrace.

Despite my multiple attempts to start a conversation with her, this little girl never uttered a single word. Eventually her mother said, "Okay, honey, let's go."

With that, the little girl hopped off my lap. As she began walking down the carpet, she suddenly stopped, turned to face me, and said, "I love you, Santa." Then she turned back around and tottered off with her mother.

As I watched the two of them walk away, I thought to myself, as I have hundreds of times since, *Yes, indeed . . . I definitely have the most wonderful job in the world.*

❄

BESIDES BEING GOOD FOR THE SOUL, BEING Santa is downright fun. My research is *toys*, for goodness' sake!

Santa Claus needs to be the ultimate expert on toys, after all, so I do lots of research. A child might come up and ask me for a perennial favorite like an American Girl doll, of which there are many kinds. I'll nod and say, "Which one?" Imagine the look on a little girl's face when I suggest that she might want Molly, who has brown hair just like she does, or Julie, who is from San Francisco where the little girl lives, or whichever new doll just came out that year. Sure, many boys want the ever-popular Optimus Prime Transformers action figure, but I need to be just as knowledgeable about Bumblebee, Wheeljack, or Starscream (just to name a few), in case I get a rogue request. I've also done my homework on the classics and know lots about the history of favorites like Barbie, G.I. Joe, and Slinky, which never fails to amaze my young visitors.

In order to keep my expert status, I constantly read up on the hot new toys online and subscribe to every toy catalog you can imagine. Throughout the year, I'll slip into the toy departments at Target, Walmart, or the big toy stores like Toys"R"Us to see what's front and center on the shelves. I try to do these visits on the sly, early in the morning or late at night, so the children don't see me.

A couple of times during the year, however, I go to the toy stores during the daytime to get an idea of what children really like, straight from the source. While I'm there—especially if it's near Christmastime—the kids inevitably mob me, even though I'm dressed in regular clothes. The funny thing is that many of them see it as an impromptu opportunity to put in their requests. I can't tell you how many times a child has walked up to me in the toy aisle, held up something they're excited about, and said matter-of-factly, "I want this one!"

❄

THEN YOU HAVE ALL THE FUN BELLS AND WHIS-
tles that go along with being Santa. As both a techie
and an actor, I get a real kick out of the Santa Claus
gear, starting with the most important piece of all: the
red suit.

My first Santa suit, as you know, was a gift from my
friends at the radio station in Charleston, South Carolina.
It didn't take me long after appearing more often as
Santa to realize that one suit was *definitely* not enough.

I often wonder how my fellow Santas and I manage
to keep our rotund body shapes with the ridiculous
amount we perspire under all those bulky layers and
fur trim during the Christmas season. If you think
about it, Santa Claus's suit needs to keep him warm as
he travels around the world during wintertime in an
open sleigh, or while he's at home in the frosty North
Pole. But once Santa walks into a nice, toasty house or
sits in front of hot camera lights, the need to bundle up
disappears, and you're left with one sizzling Santa. Fortunately, perspiration doesn't show through velvet. But
just because people don't see it doesn't mean that Santa's not baking like a rotisserie chicken inside his suit!

An overheating Santa is generally not a candy cane–
scented one, so I eventually added not one but two more
suits to my repertoire: one to wear, one as backup while
the primary one goes to the dry cleaner every three

days, and one backup to the backup in case of last-minute mishaps.

There's a whole colorful world of Santa-wear out there. I've seen candy-striped shirts, green satin tunics, and red-and-gold-checkered vests. There are short red coats with fluffy double-shawled collars, long Victorian robes in burgundy velvet with gold chain fasteners, and the old-world European version of Father Christmas with earth tones, a wreath around his head, and a walking stick. Even on the traditional Santa Claus suit, there's an impressive array of choices to make it your own: gilt-embroidered coats, customized golden Santa belt buckles, handmade leather boots, hats with holly and bells, square spectacles . . . the variety is endless.

When I worked exclusively as a mall Santa, I stuck to the classic red and white ensemble. In later years, when I did a season as a Santa-in-residence at a photography studio, I spent more time moving around and playing with kids on the floor, which meant I got even hotter. I had the freedom to dress in whatever kind of Santa Claus suit I wanted, so I figured that was the time to have some fun experimenting.

Somewhere around that time, I'd read an article about why some children are afraid of Santa in a professional Santa Claus newsletter. I discovered that one of the things that frighten children about Santa is that every inch of his body is covered (children use visual cues like body shape, hands, and the face to determine an adult's trustworthiness). So I contacted a company who specialized in custom Santa Claus outfits, and I ordered the outfit for "Workshop" Santa. Workshop Santa was a little more casual, and a whole lot less daunting.

Instead of the bulky coat and clown pants that hid my body shape, I wore red velvet bib overalls that strapped over the shoulders and came up to my mid-chest area, and a simple white dress shirt. No hat covering my head, no gloves on my hands. The costume worked out splendidly. I still had my familiar white hair and beard, but I looked as though I was ready to cobble together some new toys for them right then and there. Children seemed completely comfortable and relaxed around this workshop version of Santa, even the very littlest ones—almost no fears or tears! As for me, without the heavy coat, I could romp freely with the kids without roasting.

As a professional Santa, I get to play with all sorts of clever gadgets and inventions. Who says Santa doesn't love toys, too? I have a whole collection of special Santa colognes to spray onto my clothing in different Christmas scents like gingerbread, peppermint, pine, cinnamon, and cocoa. My GenuineSanta.com website brings Santa into the modern age and allows me to happily tinker with all kinds of technological bells and whistles. But my favorite toy, of course, is my Santamobile, which I drive year-round. It's a cherry-red Chevy with the word *Santa* painted on the sides, and it's loaded with all kinds of fun thingamabobs: neon lights around the SANTA license plates, speakers that can play Christmas music outside the car when it's parked, and synchronized strobe lights that flash to the music from underneath the chassis. Batman may have his Batmobile, but Santa Sal's car is every bit as cool, if I do say so myself.

You might wonder if all this is really necessary. And the answer, for me, is that I always want to do everything I can to be as authentic for kids as possible. It's important for me to be believable and wondrous in their eyes. If I'm wearing a flimsy belt that breaks or if my boot toppers look fake and obvious, some of the magical shine gets lost—remember Kevin, who spotted the glue-on Santa's beard and very nearly gave up believing?

And even if children are blind to the authenticity of Santa, the camera lens isn't. The pictures these families take with me will be in the family photo album for years and years, and I want those memories to hold up. One of the greatest joys for me is meeting people who care enough about Santa Claus to make him a permanent part of their recorded family history. Even more of an honor is when parents who sat on my lap a decade earlier when they were children bring their own kids to take a holiday picture with me. If it matters enough to them to continue that personal Santa connection through the generations, then it certainly matters to me that they're getting an authentic-looking (and good-smelling) Santa Claus.

❄

BEST OF ALL, I GET TO CELEBRATE CHRISTMAS cheer 365 days a year. I'll walk into the local post office here in Georgia, where I now live, and folks will stop what they're doing, look over at me, and smile. Some will even say, "Hi, Santa!" I have a theory that seeing me brings up happy memories of Christmas that I believe *everyone* has. Heck, once I was pulled over on the highway by a formidable-looking state trooper. It turned out that he didn't want to give me a ticket; he just wanted to take his picture with Santa Claus!

And of course, nearly every day I come across a child who sees me as Santa, so I make every effort to carry candy canes everywhere I go in a special crimson velvet bag. I like to buy big, well-made ones; kids expect Santa to give out real candy canes, not those fragile, penny candy things! I'll stock up on fifty boxes at a time just to make sure I always have some on hand. They go pretty quickly, especially since the parents almost always ask for one, too. And their smiles are usually just as big as their children's.

So you see, as much cheer as I might have brought to others in my role as Santa, being Santa Claus has given me more to celebrate, enjoy, and be grateful for than I ever could have imagined.

NINE

❄

The Myth of the "Perfect Christmas"

YOU HEAR IT A LOT AROUND CHRISTMASTIME: people feeling overwhelmed with too much to do, too many obligations and responsibilities, tying themselves in knots to make the holidays perfect. I'll overhear parents talking to one another while they are waiting in line to see me, saying things like "I'm running myself ragged trying to find the doll/truck/video game my child wants" or "We drove to four different places searching for the right tree." All the rushing and pressure can turn what's supposed to be the happiest season of all into the most stressful time of the year. I really do understand— even Santa sometimes finds himself stretched a little too thin, trying to be all things to everyone.

My success as a mall Santa turned out to be a mixed

blessing. Being a Santa-in-residence for an entire season was exciting for me, and, at the same time, my roster of regulars for home visits kept growing. There came one Christmas, however, when I found that I had more home visit bookings than I could fit into my schedule. My hours at the mall were running later and later, which left no way to make it to some of these families' homes before their children would go to sleep.

That presented quite a conundrum for me. As I started calling up parents to explain the problem, most sounded very disappointed and asked if I could think of some way—any way at all—to come to their house. They so wanted their children to see Santa Claus walk into their very own living rooms.

Honestly, I couldn't think of anything. I would need to be in two places at once. While the real Santa Claus might have the ability to make it to every home around the globe in a single night, I hadn't figured out how he managed that particular trick yet. If I canceled the home visits, I'd be going back on my word and disappointing dozens of children. But if I didn't show up at the mall for the hours I was scheduled, I'd be disappointing hundreds more, not to mention probably doing damage to my credibility as a reliable Santa. Suddenly I understood what people meant when they talked about holiday stress.

Stumped for a solution, I remembered a friend of mine who played Santa at a different mall. Like me, he put in long days at his North Pole Village set, but I knew he also made home visits. So I called him up and asked how he managed it.

"Pajama visits," he said.

"What's that?" I asked.

"You arrive after the children are asleep," he explained, "and the parents wake the kids up with, 'I think I hear Santa downstairs!' The children then 'discover' Santa putting presents underneath the tree."

How simple! How obvious! I would still be able to appear at many of my regular customers' houses; I'd just have to do all the visits on Christmas Eve. After all, Santa doesn't come and put presents under the tree in early December. I called back the disappointed parents and explained the pajama visit, and they loved the idea. So I scheduled as many pajama visits as I could fit in in one night, with arrival times as late as 3:00 in the morning.

However, with travel required between pajama visit locations, I quickly ran out of slots for Christmas Eve, with many of my regular customers still wanting visits. Then I thought of another idea, in its own way almost better than a pajama visit. I called it a Santa Cam visit. Admittedly, it took a bit of extra effort to set up, but if parents went along with the idea, the payoff on Christmas Day for the children would be priceless.

Here's how it worked: Weeks or even days before Christmas, the parents and I would set up a time in the morning just after their children had left for school, and before I had to leave for the mall. This gave us about ninety minutes of "safe" time when the kids wouldn't be home to catch us.

Once I arrived and got into my Santa suit, we would cover all the windows to make the room look dark and then set up the video camera on a tripod. I would put all of the presents into my sack and stand just in front of the fireplace, freezing into a crouching pose.

On my signal, the parents would press Record. With the camera now taping, I would "climb" out of the fireplace and look around. If I saw some milk and cookies left out for me, I would eat one or two, drink the milk, and then place the presents under the tree. One by one, I would take the wrapped gifts out of my sack. During this whole process, I'd hum and sing a few Christmas songs, comment on this or that piece of furniture or a picture on the wall, and even talk to some of the toys themselves, saying things like, "I heard that Pamela loves her dollies, so I'm sure you'll be really happy here."

Then, with all of the toys placed under the tree, I'd grab my sack and start walking back to the fireplace. On my way, I would suddenly "notice" the camera. I'd walk toward it and say, "Boy, I hope this thing isn't on!" I would stick my face really close to the camera lens, look shocked, and say, "Oh, my goodness! It *is* on!" Then I would touch my finger to my nose and hold still for a second while one of the parents hit the Pause button.

For the big finish, with the camera paused, I would step out of the frame and take some glitter confetti out of my pocket. On my cue, the parent would hit Record again, and I would toss the glitter at the camera. On video, it looked like Santa had vanished, leaving only a sparkle. I recommended that, before the parents put the presents away after I left, they let the camera keep filming until it ran out of tape. I knew that some of the smart kids out there would smell a trick and wonder, "Hey, why did the camera come on *only* while Santa was here and stop right after he left?" By letting the camera keep recording until the end of the tape, it would seem like something mysterious made the camera turn on just as Santa arrived, but nothing turned it off again.

Of course, to make this work, the parents' job became critically important on Christmas Eve. They needed to set up the video camera in the same spot and put a blank tape into it. And if the children asked the reason for setting the camera up the night before, the parents would explain that it was so the camera would be ready on Christmas morning to take video of all the gifts being opened.

Then, after the children went to sleep, the parents would take out the hidden presents and lay out all the gifts exactly where Santa had put them on the video-tape (we used Polaroid pictures to make sure the layout was the same). Then they would switch the blank tape for the Santa Cam tape.

In the morning, the family would come downstairs, the kids would be scrambling for the presents under the tree, and suddenly Mom or Dad would say, "Hey, this videotape has something on it! It's at the end of the tape, but I know I put a blank tape in there." The family would then rewind the tape to see what was on it, and—lo and behold—they caught Santa Claus coming out of the fireplace, eating some cookies and milk, putting presents under their tree, and then disappearing.

Some parents later told me that their children took the tapes into school for show-and-tell. I can only imagine the reactions in those classrooms.

Santa Cam visits allowed me to visit many more children than if I'd worked only on Christmas Eve. Nearly two dozen families received Santa Cam visits that year, and I still got to interact with hundreds of others at the mall in the North Pole Village. My solution may not have been perfect, but it still made for a very Merry Christmas for them—and a whole lot less stress for Santa!

❋

THE FUNNY THING ABOUT TRYING TO MAKE Christmas perfect for our kids, I've come to realize, is that that's not what really matters to them. Sure, they want toys and stockings stuffed with goodies, but what they really, truly want is that magical Christmas feeling. And love is the biggest component. As long as love is there, the Christmas spirit comes through. I've seen families work extra-long hours to make the holiday special for their children, but often they tell me that the most priceless moments they have are seeing their children's faces when they meet Santa. It's the sharing of these treasured moments that makes Christmas special.

I'm not one to give advice, but if I were, I would say to parents: slow down and take a breath. Put aside the high-pressure sales, the search for the biggest and best tree, and the mythical idea of what a "perfect Christmas" looks like. And simply spend time together as a family, enjoying the Christmas spirit in the air. It's free, you know! Sit down and watch some of the classic or funny Christmas movies on television together, or take a walk down a city street lit up with twinkling lights and stroll past the festive store windows. As I learned from the invention of the Santa Cam, children don't need "perfect" to have a Merry Christmas. There are a million different ways to give them the wonder of the holiday without running yourself ragged. And if you don't get it exactly perfect . . . well, children appreciate our best efforts more than we might think.

Take it from Santa: the simple, special moments of togetherness are what create the most lasting Christmas memories.

TEN

The Reason for the Season

AS MUCH AS I WISH THAT LIFE AS A PROFESSIONAL Santa Claus was always filled with smiles and sparkles, that's not necessarily the case. One of the things that happens is that I—along with other Santas I know—take a lot of flak about the commercialization of Christmas.

There are folks who feel that Christmas has become nothing more than an excuse for retailers to whip shoppers into a frenzy in order to make more money. They look around at the fancy decorations, the 5:00 A.M. sale madness, and other holiday trappings and despair that the spirit of Christmas has gotten lost amid all the "stuff." Some even get angry that the holiday festivities start as early as the first week of November, and I suppose Santa is a relatively easy target. I've actually had people walk up to me while I was doing an appearance at a shopping center and say, "Shame on you for being at the mall before Thanksgiving!"

But from my perspective, people are looking at this in the wrong way. They see Santa's November appearances as nothing more than retailers looking to rush the season to make more money. I can't speak for all Santas, but as for me, I see myself being out there simply to get people into the spirit of Christmas. When is it ever too soon to feel joyful?

It saddens me that people believe that Santa or Christmas have become somehow tainted. From my perspective, when people say Christmas is too commercialized, it's because they, in their hearts, have allowed it to become that way. We all have to define things for ourselves. It took a shaking of my own faith for me to learn that it's up to each one of us to decide what Christmas is truly all about.

❅

THE YEAR 2007 WAS NOT A GREAT ONE FOR Santa Claus.

The cultural feeling toward Christmas and Santa had begun shifting. A growing number of news articles that year reported how big chain stores were no longer allowing their greeters to say "Merry Christmas," replacing it with the more politically correct "Happy Holidays" or "Season's Greetings." And then, shortly after

Thanksgiving, the acting surgeon general of the United States made the following comment to the *Boston Herald*: "It is really important that the people who kids look up to as role models are in good shape, eating well and getting exercise . . . Santa is no different."

Reporters and radio hosts quickly found my website and flooded me with calls and requests for my reaction. "How does it make you feel knowing that the surgeon general thinks Santa Claus is a bad role model for children?" they asked. "Do you think the United States has declared war on Christmas?"

I always provided them with honest answers. During most interviews, I would say, "In all my years playing Santa Claus, I've had a lot of children sit on my lap and tell me what they want to be when they grow up. I've heard fireman, astronaut, ballerina, baseball player, rock star, doctor, comic book artist, video game maker, and even president of the United States. But no child has ever told me, 'I want to be you, Santa.' I think they realize that there's only one Santa Claus. So I can't imagine that children want to be fat just so they can be more like Santa."

As I did more and more interviews, I found out that public controversies surrounding Santa Claus extended beyond just the United States. The Australian government had recently discouraged their Santas from saying "Ho, ho, ho!" because the word "ho" had developed a negative slang meaning. The government urged their

Australian Santas to say "Ha, ha, ha!" instead. I kid you not.

In merry old England, concerns about pedophilia had led Rotary Clubs throughout the United Kingdom to bar children from sitting on Santa's lap. The citizens of Great Britain now had to take photos of their children sitting *next to* Santa Claus.

Unbelievable! Preposterous! When did Santa Claus become an international villain?

I suppose I shouldn't have been shocked. There had also been rumblings of yuletide unhappiness the prior season in 2006 when, for the first time as Santa, I found myself faced with a few unpleasant experiences. The first was being told by a mall's corporate representative that if I wanted to return as their Santa-in-residence that year, I would have to do it exclusively—meaning that I couldn't appear in families' homes. But I already had more than a dozen appearances scheduled. Many of my regular customers had booked me well in advance to do personal appearances, and my pajama visits had gone so well that several others had reserved me specifically for Christmas Eve.

When I explained to this representative that I wouldn't be able to agree to exclusivity, she replied rather nastily, "Mr. Lizard, these are the terms. You are free to take them or leave them. Frankly, we can dress up any person with a white beard as Santa Claus, and people will still come to see him."

That statement shocked me speechless. I thought of all the little things I'd done to make my appearances as Santa extra special: singing songs with people while they waited in line, getting out of my chair and changing location to help the children who were afraid of Santa, the research I did on the latest toys, all the ways that I'd answer tough questions from kids. To this day, I have no idea whether the woman's statement reflected a corporate philosophy or simply her own opinion about Santas being all alike. Regardless, I felt hurt, angry, and to be quite honest, disgusted.

"Thank you," I managed to say. "But I think I'll pass this year."

As it happened, I got a call a few weeks later from my old friends at Photo Promotions offering me a season-long Santa Claus role at a mall in Massachusetts. They did not require an exclusive contract. They also didn't need me for the same full-time commitment.

Although fewer hours meant less money, it opened up my schedule to book appearances at day care centers, nursing homes, office Christmas parties, and of course, home visits before Christmas. I'd be doing a lot more driving, but the opportunity to make so many personal appearances outside of the hustle and bustle of the mall environment enlivened my Christmas spirit.

Unfortunately, I quickly discovered that the Photo Promotions people had become quite concerned that camera phone photos of Santa Claus would cut into their sales. My group sing-a-longs with people waiting in line were no longer allowed because there would be no way to prevent mall patrons from snapping pictures and videos of Santa leading the chorus. What's more, whenever I went on a break, Photo Promotions insisted I could only walk to my dressing room accompanied by a helper who would make certain that no one took my picture along the way.

Another change also didn't sit well with me: I had to remain seated constantly while on the Santa set. Even with no line and nobody waiting to sit on Santa's lap, I had to stay in my chair, or at least not walk anywhere beyond the white fences in order to prevent random photos from being taken by passersby.

I still did what I could to interact with people while remaining seated. I would wave and smile at people coming down the escalator toward the set. During slow times when no one sat on my lap and a family walked past, I would give a hearty "Ho, ho, ho!" From my chair, I even made friends with the mall walkers who came to the mall to do their exercise. I could always spot mall walkers because they would do laps around the mall, over and over again. With some of them, each time they would pass by the Santa set, I would hold up fingers to keep count for them of how many laps they had done and then give them a smile.

Even so, despite reaching out with grins and winks and ho-ho-ho's, things felt off for me. Besides feeling uncomfortable with the new policies of my employer, I sensed a kind of pall in the air. The helpers seemed less happy. The parents appeared more stressed and less patient. Many of the stores had already replaced the traditional MERRY CHRISTMAS signs with more politically correct HAPPY HOLIDAYS signs.

Then I experienced something that had never happened to me in all my years of being Santa Claus. Shortly after Thanksgiving, I drove about ninety minutes across Massachusetts to appear at a family's Christmas party. They'd made the reservation months earlier, telling me to expect a large number of kids along with relatives and friends of relatives. I had reserved up to two hours for this visit, since that many children meant countless photos and lots of Christmas lists to hear, and I didn't want to rush anything.

As I drove into the neighborhood where the hosts lived, I saw cars parked all along the street leading up to the brightly lit house. *Wow, this is quite a party,* I thought with a little smile. *This is going to be fun!* I temporarily double-parked in order to dial the parents' phone number, tell them I had arrived, and ask how they would like to announce my entrance.

"Oh, crap!" I heard the woman on the line say to me. Then, slightly muffled as she turned her voice away from the phone, "Honey! Can you come deal with this? That Santa we hired is outside." I heard some arguing, and then the woman said, "My husband will be right out."

A few seconds later, a man in a sweater walked over to my car. I got out to introduce myself, but before I could say anything, he started talking. "Look, I'm really sorry you had to come out here. My wife was supposed to cancel you."

"Cancel me?" I asked, confused. "But it looks like you're having your party."

"Yeah, we are," the husband looked annoyed and clearly wanted to get this over with. "But it's not a Christmas party. It's a holiday party. We've got some Jewish friends, there's an atheist boyfriend, I even think a couple of my daughter's friends are Buddhists—anyway, having Santa Claus just wouldn't be appropriate this year."

He offered to pay for my gas, but quickly added that they wouldn't be paying my fee. I thought about arguing with him, but I respect the red suit, and I firmly believe that Santa Claus wouldn't ever make a scene. So I got back into my car and started the long return trip back home. Three hours' round-trip driving on a cold night just to be told they didn't want Santa Claus at their party after all.

It turns out this exception to the rule suddenly became anything but.

Just a few days later, I had my second last-minute cancellation at the door of a visit. Yet again, a Christmas party had somehow turned into a "holiday" party, and having Santa there would be politically incorrect.

Before that Christmas season had finished, I found myself with nearly a dozen last-minute cancellations, each one due to the shift from Christmas to a more generic holiday party. Santa would not be needed. And no one—not one client—would pay for the visit that they now did not want. The tightening economy had turned Christmas giving into an epidemic of tight frugality, and not even a man dressed as Santa Claus could relieve people of that mind-set.

After so many years of doing business as Santa Claus on little more than a friendly voice and a verbal handshake over the telephone, I sadly realized things needed to change. With a heavy heart, I changed my website to require customers to place a nonrefundable deposit. I'd never required a deposit before. But once I book an appearance, that time slot is reserved and no longer available to others who might also want a visit from Santa. By canceling at the last minute, these people didn't just inconvenience me—they also hurt other families who weren't able to have me visit their home.

Being Santa Claus had always seemed simpler and more personal to me than my usual business deals. Santa Claus had held a special place for me, away from the need for contracts and billing procedures. Now, however, it seemed like the business of Santa was indeed becoming something else entirely.

Nevertheless, I went into the Christmas season of 2007 once again filled with excitement. Despite all the

unpleasantness of the prior season and the Santa back-
lash caused by the surgeon general's statement, I still
felt hopeful that Christmas cheer would prevail for me.
Photo Promotions had hired me back for regular shifts
at the mall, and I had a full schedule of visits to homes,
day care facilities, offices, and recreation centers. But
that feeling didn't last long. As it turned out, I was
about to hit my lowest point.

It happened just a few days before Christmas, as I
finished up my shift at the mall. I walked to my car
and saw shattered glass all over the asphalt next to the
driver's-side window.

It took me a moment to process the scene. And then
I realized with a weight sinking into the pit of my stomach: someone had broken into my car. I looked around
for my possessions, only to discover that thieves had
stolen almost everything inside—including a GPS system, my laptop computer, a video camcorder, a power
converter, my cell phone charger . . . and my spare Santa
Claus outfit.

"Who would steal from Santa Claus?!"

The police officer that arrived at the scene tried to
assure me that many cars get broken into at the mall, so
he doubted mine was specifically targeted. But I knew
there was no way the thieves didn't know they were
breaking into Santa's car. The car had a bobblehead
Santa on the dashboard, holly leaves clipped to the
rearview mirror, and my Santa suit hung from the clip

in the backseat. Anyone scoping out the parking garage would see the old guy with the beard getting out, figure he was the Santa Claus for the mall, and know they had about four hours clear to break into his car before he came back out.

I naïvely believed that even the worst of crooks would have at least a little respect for Santa Claus and not break into his vehicle. Apparently not. It sickened me to imagine this thief putting on my Santa suit to hand out all those "gifts" he had just stolen from me.

"Oh, Linda, the world's become an awful, awful place," I grumbled to my wife that evening. I felt violated, angry, and depressed. Christmas wasn't fun anymore. It had turned into something awful and ugly for me. This wasn't the kind of Christmas I wanted to be associated with.

"I'll tell you this much, Linda," I said. "This is the last year I work as a mall Santa. I might not even play Santa Claus at all next year."

"Now, Sal, try not to make any decisions while you're so angry. Things could be very different next year."

"I doubt it." I sighed. "It just seems to get worse and worse. Maybe there's a certain type of person who's meant to be Santa Claus, and I'm beginning to wonder if that's me."

"Well, why don't you finish out this last week and we'll talk about it then," Linda said, trying to sound positive. "A lot could still happen . . ."

Linda and I said our good nights, and I went to sleep, praying for some kind of guidance as I closed my eyes.

The next morning, I bundled up and—still feeling miserable—drove to the auto body shop with the heat turned up to try to lessen the impact of the snow blowing in through the missing side window. I picked up a rental car for the day and headed back to the mall, taking what few valuables I had left with me.

As I reached the end of my shift, the mall crowd began thinning out as the stores started to close for the night. I got up from my chair, said good night to my helpers, and headed for my dressing room.

As I closed the gate of the white picket fence behind me, an older woman walked up to me from the side and said, "Excuse me . . ."

I turned and smiled at her. "Yes, dear, what can I do for you?"

"Do you make personal appearances?" she asked me.

"Yes, I do," I told her. "But this close to Christmas, my schedule is pretty booked. I don't have a lot of openings left."

She looked disappointed. But with a flash of hope, she said, "Well, I don't think it will take very long . . ."

"Is it some kind of house visit?" I asked.

She chuckled. "Well, yes, I suppose it is. God's house, actually. It's for my church."

I had made a few church appearances in the past. I'd handed out Christmas presents to children after services back in South Carolina. "Well, ma'am," I said as kindly as I could, "if it's at a church, there will probably be a lot of children wanting to sit on my lap and take pictures with me. I'm not sure it'll be that brief of an appearance."

"Oh, you won't need to do any of that," she said.

"I won't?"

"I have this gift," she said, holding out a wrapped present. "It's for the church. I just want you to come in after services begin on Christmas Eve and place it on the altar. You don't have to stay or say anything. Just leave the present and you can walk back out again."

I thought about this unusual request. I felt a little unsure about Santa Claus walking into the middle of a religious service. I didn't want to seem disrespectful or make anyone feel awkward. And to be honest, I'd scheduled a full night of pajama visits and wasn't entirely certain I'd be able to squeeze in even a brief appearance at her church.

As I started to regretfully apologize and say no, I looked into this woman's hopeful eyes and couldn't bring myself to disappoint her. I asked for the address of the church and, coincidentally enough, it was located rather close to a few of my scheduled visits for Christmas Eve. As it happened, I would easily be able to make an appearance at the beginning of their 9:00 P.M. service.

"Okay, I'll be there," I said.

"Oh, thank you so very much!" she said, and she handed me the present and gave me a kiss on the cheek.

I arrived at the small church a few minutes early on a snowy and frigid Christmas Eve. As I sat there in the back of the parking lot, dressed in full Santa garb and waiting for everyone to enter the church, I still felt a little nervous. But when the clock on my dashboard turned to 9:01, I reminded myself that I had made a promise, and so I reached over to grab the woman's gift from the passenger seat and got out of my car.

My boots crunched in the snow with every stride as I walked up to the doors of the church. I could hear the organ music from inside getting louder, and I could see the flickering light of the candles through the stained glass windows.

I opened one of the doors and stepped inside. The church felt warm compared to the blustery night outside, and as I stood there quietly looking at the backs of the seated congregation, I wondered when would be a good time to walk up the aisle. Should I wait for the music to stop? I worried I might inadvertently interrupt a prayer, so I decided to head up while the organist still played.

As I began silently walking up the center aisle, I realized that no one had seen me standing in the back. But with each step, more and more people noticed me. And of course, it's hard to miss the bright crimson coat of Santa Claus in the middle of a church.

Heads began turning and craning to look at me. More and more voices started to whisper to each other. When I was about halfway to the altar, the organ music stopped playing and the voices dropped to a hush. As I took my last few steps, all I could hear were the echoes of my boots on the floor, filling the chamber.

And then silence. Absolute silence as two hundred people stared at me from every corner of that huge room. I felt rather self-conscious in a way I seldom do when wearing the red suit. But as I looked up to see the statue of a blessed man on a cross above me, I suddenly felt a strange and wonderful peace. All the sadness, anger, and disillusionment instantaneously melted away. I knelt down before the altar, bowed my head, and placed the woman's present gently on the floor.

My task complete, I stood up, turned around, and quietly began walking out of the church the way I had come in. As I moved up the aisle, I glanced around through the congregation, seeing if I could spot the face of the woman who had hired me. I couldn't find her, but as I walked past row after row of churchgoers, I noticed many of the women and even some of the men had started to cry. Somehow I knew these were tears of joy, of hope and faith and reassurance.

I can't know for certain what all of these people thought and felt that night, and yet a part of me did know as I looked into all of those faces. These people had seen the news reports of the surgeon general's

Santa Claus warning (the story had permeated the headlines all over New England). Like me, they all knew that saying "Merry Christmas" had become unfashionable. Like me, these believers in Christmas had begun to wonder if the meaning of this special holiday was somehow slipping away, getting lost among growing greed and paranoia and everything that Christmas shouldn't represent.

And then Santa Claus had appeared in their church. He didn't say "Ho, ho, ho." He didn't try to sell a product or charge for a photo or even ask for a donation to some charity. He simply did what Santa always does: he gave a present. He put it at the feet of someone very special. And for a brief moment, Santa reminded the people in that church of what Christmas had always been about.

Yes, the world had gone a little crazy. Many people of all faiths had lost their way. But as I walked up that aisle, I felt a wave of love and goodwill moving through me from everyone in that congregation. In that instant, we all found the faith to know in our hearts that the temporary insanity of the world would somehow pass.

By the time I got back into my car, I realized that I had tears in my eyes, too. I knew that the world would start believing in the goodness of Santa Claus again. Santa wasn't a villain. "Merry Christmas" wasn't a forbidden phrase never to be uttered out of fear of political incorrectness. Christmas was more than just a religious holiday or an excuse to eat too many candy canes. Christmas was a state of mind.

I finished my remaining pajama visits that night. And as I drove back home, I knew deep down that I could never give up being Santa Claus, no matter what the world might throw at me. The celebration of Christmas itself had become too much a part of my being to ever walk away.

❄

SO THESE DAYS, WHENEVER I HEAR SOMEONE grumble or complain about the commercialization of Christmas, I encourage them to focus on the real reason for the season. Whether you're Christian, Jewish, Muslim, Buddhist, or anything else, the essential element is faith. Faith in families, faith that we can create peace on earth, faith in love. To me, whatever we believe in and cherish is what we want to make Christmas about. The true meaning of the holiday can never get lost if we keep that spirit of Christmas alive in our hearts.

ELEVEN

The Spinach Cookie Story

BY 2008, I'D DECIDED TO GIVE MY ROLE AS A mall Santa a rest. It had been a great run, despite the bumps in the road of the past two seasons, but I sensed it was time to try a new adventure. I wanted to do something that allowed me the more personal interactions I enjoyed during my home visits and in-person appearances. My experience in the church had restored my faith, and now what I needed to nurse my newly revived Christmas spirit was the best medicine of all: the sweet sound of children laughing.

And so I accepted a job as a Santa-in-residence at a very friendly, enterprising photography studio that was set up inside a mall but wasn't part of the mall operation itself. It was perfect for me—all of the festivity with none of the high-pressured rushing.

I loved the shop's warm, wonderful atmosphere. The

staff there was thrilled when I offered to get down on the floor to play with a stubborn toddler in order to give him a chance to warm up to me and take a happy picture. I did this a few times in different ways with different children, and by my second day, the photographers no longer bothered trying to pose me with the kids. I would simply interact with them in whatever ways seemed most comfortable for them, and the photographer would follow the action and get a series of precious candid pictures.

It helped that I would start playing with the children while they were still in the waiting area, as I hung out there between portrait sessions. I did funny Santa voices and we sang songs together. I'd like to say that it was all for the benefit of the kids, but really, I was having an equally good time! This kind of lighthearted merriment was *exactly* what this Santa needed. I felt relaxed, happy, and inspired to have fun again, which is how the spinach cookie story came to be.

Children love to be told stories, and, I figured, who better to tell a tale than Santa Claus himself? So while driving home one night, I came up with a story that I could tell to children while they were waiting for their parents to choose picture styles and pay before the photo session began. Since then, I've told this story probably hundreds of times, and to this day it remains the most frequently requested of all my Santa Claus tales.

It goes like this . . .

As the children sit around me, usually cross-legged on the floor in a circle, I ask them, "Do you want to hear the story about the *spinach cookie*?"

They shout, "YES!"

"Well, you know, kids always ask me what's my favorite kind of cookie, because they want to know what kind of cookies to leave out for me when I visit them on Christmas Eve. Now, who here likes chocolate chip cookies?" A few children will raise their hands. "How many of you like Oreo cookies?" A few more will raise their hands. "How about gingerbread cookies? Christmas sugar cookies? Do you like the ones with the M&M's in 'em?" By this point, all the children have probably raised their hands multiple times.

"So you can see just how hard it is for me to make up *my* mind when children ask what's my favorite cookie. But I *can* tell you the story of the *worst* cookie I ever ate. It was about—oh, I don't know—maybe fifty years ago. Which seems like a long time to all of you, but it's just the blink of an eye to me. There was this little girl named Molly—she was about six or seven years old at the time—and she lived in a small town in Ohio. One day, Molly visited me at the mall with her parents, sat on my knee, and told me that she wanted an Easy-Bake Oven for Christmas.

"And I said, 'What are you going to use the Easy-Bake Oven for?' I figured she was going to say that she would help bake things for her family. But instead, she said, 'If you leave me an Easy-Bake Oven, Santa, I'll use it to make you some Christmas cookies! They'll be the *best* cookies you ever had, I promise!'

"Ho, ho, ho!" At this point in the story, I always laugh and look around at all the children. "You all know how much I like cookies! So I saw this as a chance to make a little investment. That year, I left Molly an Easy-Bake Oven. And you know what happened?

"I came back to visit the next year, and as I'm putting presents underneath Molly's tree, I look over to notice, right next to the fireplace, there was a little table sitting there with milk and cookies on it.

"Well, you know how much I love cookies and milk! So I hurried to put all the presents under the tree, and all the time I was thinking about how good those cookies were going to taste. Once I was finished with the presents, I went over to the table and saw a note next to the cookies. And the note said: 'Dear Santa, I made you these cookies with my Easy-Bake Oven. I hope you like them. Thank you so much! Love, Molly.'

"And I thought, 'How sweet of Molly to remember that she promised to make me Christmas cookies.' So I took off my glove, reached over, and picked up the first cookie. It looked so good and I was so excited to taste it. And then I put it in my mouth and bit down into the *worst* cookie I ever tasted. Do you know why?"

And everyone will ask, "Why?"

"Molly made spinach cookies!"

A giant chorus of "EWWWWWW!!!" invariably follows.

And I reply, "That's what I said! You know, spinach is good for you, and cookies are good, but the two of them should *never* be put together. So I just couldn't eat it. But I didn't want to break Molly's heart because she was such a sweet little girl to think of me. So you know what I did? I drank the glass of milk, and I took the cookies with me up the chimney. When I got to the roof, I broke them up into pieces and fed them to the reindeer. But it turns out that wasn't the smartest thing I ever did. You know why?"

"Why?" they ask, their little eyes wide with anticipation.

"Spinach gives reindeer gas!" And the children all laugh because nothing in the world is funnier to a child than a good toot.

"And so I called them all by name: On Dasher! On Dancer! And all of a sudden, I hear *PLBTTTT*!!!" and I make a raspberry noise with my tongue and lips. "And I said, 'Wait a minute, what was that?' I looked around, because I'm wondering if somebody had hopped into my sleigh. But I didn't see anybody. So I continued, 'On Prancer! On Vixen!' and I hear another *PLBTTTT*!!! And that's when I realized it was the *reindeer*.

"And oh, the *smell!* It wasn't a good one, if you know what I mean. It didn't smell like cookies! And I had to ride around the entire world all night long smelling reindeer toots!" By this point, the children are rolling around on the floor laughing, and I'm usually having a hard time keeping a straight face myself.

In all the years I've been telling this story, the funny-bone tickling sound of children's giggles never fails to do my heart good. Sharing a laugh with kids is a delightful way to put the merry back into one's Christmas!

TWELVE

❄

Papá Noel the Taxi Driver

PEOPLE ASK ME ALL KINDS OF QUESTIONS about being Santa Claus, from how many pajama visits I can squeeze into a single Christmas Eve (more than a dozen) to how often I have to trim my beard (about three times a year). I'm always happy to answer any question about my Santa adventures, and most are pretty easy. But as the country headed into a recession, I found myself being asked some interesting questions about the role of Santa in tough times that made me stop and think.

One recent conversation in particular stands out in my mind. An acquaintance of mine had read an article discussing the effect that the tightening economy had on children at Christmas. She asked me, "Have kids changed what they tell you they want for Christmas?"

At first I wasn't sure what she meant. "You mean, are there different kinds of toys out there?"

"No, no," she explained. "I mean, with the economy and all, do they ask for fewer toys, or do the parents take you aside and tell you to try to steer their kids away from expensive gifts for Christmas? I've been reading that these kinds of things are happening, and I'm curious what you've seen."

I thought about it for a few moments. To be honest, I hadn't really noticed any change in the kinds of things kids had been asking me for. And no parent has ever told me to steer their child toward fewer presents or less expensive toys on their Christmas list. I guess I should have expected that, given the state of the world and all, but surprisingly, it never happened.

In my personal life, I've certainly had plenty of friends over the years who have tightened their own belts in order to give their children a few extra goodies on Christmas. Heck, I've even had to do it myself in lean times. But as Santa, I've never—not once—had a parent even mention their finances to me. No matter what might be going on for them behind the scenes, when I'm there visiting with their children, they seem to put their worries on hold for a bit and simply enjoy seeing their kids have fun with Santa.

I think that for both children and parents, Santa Claus represents a welcome distraction from the harsher realities of life that many of us have to deal with. Children can tell Santa Claus their hopes and dreams the same way they might wish upon a star. And most parents wouldn't ever want to dash those dreams or put limits on their children's innocent optimism. Even in tough economic times—perhaps especially then—Christmas and Santa Claus represent a shining ray of hope. Sure, Santa might not give a child everything he or she wants, and honestly, I don't think that many children truly expect that. To their little minds, though, it can't hurt to at least ask, right?

But what happens when a parent has no money *at all* to spend on any Christmas toys, when even a tree or a wreath is a distant and unrealistic dream? I met someone like this several years ago, someone who needed more than just a little Christmas magic. She needed a full-on Christmas miracle from Santa Claus himself.

❄

ALTHOUGH THE ECONOMIC RECESSION WOULDN'T officially hit for another few years, there were still many folks struggling financially back in 2003. In fact, my family was among them. I no longer owned any small businesses, and the technology company I had worked for the year before had downsized a large number of employees, including me.

My Christmas season Santa Claus appearances wouldn't kick into gear for another couple of months, so

I got myself a job driving a cab. It wasn't a high-paying job, but it did help keep food on the table, and the hours were somewhat flexible. My fares seemed generally agreeable and friendly, especially to a driver who looked like Santa Claus. Of course, many times the folks in my cab didn't even see my face because it was either nighttime or simply because the back of my head faced them for most of the ride.

However, sprinkled throughout my runs came a smattering of regular customers whom I got the chance to know a little better—including one that would help make my Christmas that year very memorable.

On a chilly morning run in early November, my dispatcher sent me to one of the poorer neighborhoods in town. As I arrived in front of a large apartment complex, I saw a young woman walk out, holding the hand of a small girl who looked about four years old.

"Are you Donna?" I asked through the open passenger window.

"Yes." She had a slight Spanish accent, but her English was perfect. "We are making two stops, the first to drop off my daughter at her grandmother's and then I'll be heading to work."

"Sounds good," I said, as they both slid into the backseat.

More often than not, my adult passengers wouldn't bother to look at their taxi driver. But the children always did, and I would often catch a glimpse in my rearview mirror of the younger ones staring at me, especially as it got closer to Christmas. While many of my fellow cab drivers often complained about unruly kids acting hyper in their backseats, the children in my cab always seemed to be on their best behavior.

As we drove away from Donna's home that morning, I noticed her adorable little girl gazing at me intently. She never said a word, but I could see her big chocolate-brown eyes glued to my face the entire time. We dropped the girl off at her grandmother's house, and I drove Donna to work without much conversation. Sometimes my passengers didn't want any chitchat, and I respected their privacy. I dropped her off in front of a sandwich shop in a local strip mall, about twenty minutes from where she lived. I found out later from my dispatcher that Donna and her daughter went through this ritual every morning, since there weren't any buses that traveled anywhere near that strip mall, and Donna didn't own a car. In the evenings, the taxi company would dispatch another cab to pick up Donna from work, go get her daughter, and then drive them both back home.

A week later, my dispatcher sent me once again to pick up Donna and her daughter. As with the previous trip, I could see the little girl staring at me, even though she still didn't say a word. This time, when I stopped at the grandmother's house, I turned around and smiled at my passengers. "Okay, first stop!" I said. The little girl smiled back shyly, still saying nothing.

When Donna returned to the taxi after walking the little girl inside, she told me, "My daughter thinks you are Papá Noel."

I knew that Papá Noel was how folks referred to Santa Claus in Spanish-speaking cultures. "I get that a lot," I said. "She's a beautiful little girl. What's her name?"

"Ashley," she said.

"Oh, really? What a coincidence! I have a daughter named Ashley, too, although mine is a teenager now."

"I am afraid my Ashley will turn into a teenager before I know it," she said. "They grow up so quickly, don't they?"

"You can say that again!" I agreed, and we spent the rest of the ride swapping stories about our identically named daughters.

Luck of the draw determined which fares a taxi driver would be dispatched to pick up, and I had only a few runs with Donna and Ashley over the next few weeks. Each time, little Ashley sat there quietly staring at Papá Noel driving her to her grandmother's house. But Donna and I enjoyed chatting with each other. Despite what I imagined to be somewhat difficult life circumstances, Donna was warm, friendly, and thoroughly positive in her outlook on life.

On the morning of December 23, I got a call to pick up Donna and Ashley again. But this time, something seemed noticeably different. I sensed a cloud of sadness around Donna when I picked the two of them up. As we drove away from Donna's mother's house—with Ashley and her grandmother waving good-bye to the taxi—Donna started to cry.

I slowed down and turned around briefly to face her, "What's wrong, Donna? Are you okay?"

Donna tried to hold back her tears. "Oh, it's nothing. I'm all right." But the words were swallowed by a choked sob.

I pulled over so I could hand her a box of tissues that I had sitting on the front passenger seat.

"Thank you," she said, wiping her eyes. "It's just that I look at Ashley and feel so awful that she won't have a Christmas."

"No Christmas? Why?"

Donna seemed hesitant to share her problems with a total stranger, but after a few moments, she composed herself. "Ashley's father gives us nothing, no child support . . . nothing. So I have to work long hours just to feed us. With the busy Christmas season, the sandwich shop is open longer, and I take all the extra shifts I can. Every day I work from 8:00 in the morning to 9:00 at night. Then I pick up Ashley and take her home to put her to bed. So now I work seven days a week, and I have no time to buy Ashley any Christmas presents. Not that I could even afford to if I did. Even with the extra shifts, there's no money at all this year for extras. We don't even have a tree. It's so unfair for her not to have a Christmas, but I can't afford not to work . . . even for one shift."

I felt so awful. I tried to tell her that everything would be all right and that Ashley had people who loved her, which was the most important thing. But deep down, my heart broke for them.

I dropped Donna off at work and wished her a Merry Christmas as best I could manage. But I couldn't stop thinking about Donna and her daughter missing Christmas. It all seemed so wrong.

When I got home that night and our family sat down for dinner, Linda turned to me. "Sal, you look like you're deep in thought."

I lifted my head from the plate I'd been staring at and said, "Y'know, sometimes I just wish I could be the real Santa."

"What do you mean?" she asked.

"Well, today I was in my cab, and I picked up this fare . . . ," and I went on to tell Linda and my Ashley all about Donna and her Ashley, and how this sweet little girl wouldn't have any Christmas presents because her mom was working so many hours for so little money.

"Y'know what?" our Ashley said, hopping up from the table, once again amazing Linda and me with her generous spirit. "I've got some old things from when I was little. There's books and some toys and a whole bunch of stuffed animals. In fact, I think a few of those stuffed animals even have the name Ashley sewn into them." She ran out to the garage and started hunting through boxes.

Linda turned to me. "We could probably give her some money, too, Sal."

I let the idea float around in my mind for a moment before replying, "I kinda got the feeling from her that she wouldn't accept a handout. She seems very proud. And to be honest, we really don't have a lot of money to be giving away at the moment either."

"How about we just buy them a Christmas tree, then?" Linda suggested. And in that instant, a wonderful plan started coming together, almost fully formed from the moment it entered my mind.

We needed to find a Christmas tree merchant close to where Donna lived. As it happened, there was one nearly around the corner from Donna's apartment. Fortunately, even though it had gotten pretty late, we saw the vendor still open when we drove up, probably for last-minute Christmas shoppers like us.

I told the man there that I would be buying the tree that night, but I wouldn't pick it up until mid-morning the next day. And when Linda explained to him that we were giving the tree as a surprise to a family that couldn't afford to have Christmas, the man threw in a wreath along with the tree and said both would be ready for pickup the next day.

Once we got back home, I made a very important call to the taxi company dispatcher. "Hi, Ron, it's Sal

Lizard," I said. "I need to ask you for a big favor. I'm going to start my shift early at 6:00 A.M. tomorrow, but don't send me on any calls before 6:30 because I want to pick up that woman and her daughter who we pick up and drop off every day."

"Why?" Ron sounded quite suspicious. Requests like this were frowned upon. Calls got assigned randomly or based on a taxi's location at any specific time. If drivers were allowed to request specific fares, they would likely try to get the good tippers or the easy runs. Asking to be sent to pick up a regular customer, as I was now doing, would raise a major red flag.

"Well, Ron," I explained. "The woman told me earlier today that she didn't have any Christmas presents to give her daughter this year. So my daughter has put together a bag of her old toys to give them. But tomorrow is Christmas Eve, and so tomorrow morning will be my last chance to get those presents to her before it's too late. If I can pick her up in the morning, I can give her the presents before I drop her off."

Even Ron got in on the excitement and agreed to bend the rules just this once. At 6:00 the following morning, I put on my red Santa hat to wear for the day and drove my cab over to Donna's apartment, the bag of toys hidden from sight in the trunk so Donna's Ashley wouldn't see them.

Shortly after 6:30, I heard the dispatcher's voice on the radio: "Cab 33, your call came in."

A few minutes later, Donna and Ashley came downstairs and got into my cab. Ashley saw me in my red hat, and her jaw dropped open for a second, then she broke into a big grin.

After we dropped off Ashley and headed for the strip mall, I started a casual conversation. "Do you remember I told you that I have a daughter named Ashley, too?"

"Yes," she said with a smile.

"Well, last night I told my Ashley that your Ashley wasn't going to have any presents for Christmas. So my Ashley collected a whole bunch of her old toys, most of which are in very good condition. Some of them even have the name Ashley on them. Anyway, I've got them all in a bag in the trunk, and we'd like to give them to you so you'll have presents for Ashley tomorrow on Christmas."

Donna was silent for a few seconds, as her mind seemed to be trying to process all that I'd just told her. "Are you joking?" she asked in a shocked, disbelieving voice.

"No, I'm absolutely serious," I said and smiled. "My family wants your family to have a Merry Christmas."

Suddenly, I felt her reach over the seat to give me a huge hug. Fortunately, we were stopped at a red light. She hugged me so tightly, I almost couldn't breathe.

"Oh, thank you! Thank you so much! Thank you, thank you, thank you," she said over and over again.

When we got to our destination, I opened the trunk for her. I suddenly worried that the bag—very large and quite full—might be too much for Donna to carry all by herself. But she helped me get it out and didn't seem to care about the size.

"I can't afford much, but let me at least give you something for all these presents," she said, taking out her wallet from her purse.

"Oh, you don't understand," I said quickly. "These are a gift, from my Ashley to your Ashley. Put your wallet away. I don't even want you paying for today's taxi ride. That's my gift for you."

Donna began to cry.

I started moving to get the box of tissues when she threw her arms around me and hugged me even tighter than before. "Thank you, thank you, thank you . . . ," she whispered in a quivering voice. I hugged her back. "You are an angel," she said. And then she paused. "No, your daughter is an angel. *You* are Papá Noel!" and she smiled as the tears ran down her cheeks.

I watched Donna carry the bag of toys into the back of the sandwich shop as I started driving away. It was only 7:30, and I still had a bit of work to do. My Christmas mission wasn't completed just yet.

I drove back to the Christmas tree lot by Donna's apartment, picked up the tree and wreath, and put both into the trunk. The tree stuck out, and I had to drive with the trunk open. Fortunately, I didn't need to go far.

Of course, my biggest challenge still lay ahead of me: getting into the building and delivering the tree and wreath. Thanks to the dispatcher, I knew Donna's apartment number was 214. So I waited outside the front door of her building until someone came out. During the daytime of Christmas Eve, almost no one gave a second glance to a fellow who looked like Santa with a red and white velvet hat carrying a Christmas tree and wreath. The person who came out even held the door open for me and wished me a Merry Christmas.

Once at Donna's apartment, I leaned the tree against the door, placed the wreath on the floor mat, and taped a note to the door that read, "For Apartment 214. Merry Christmas."

I exited the building and returned to my cab, feeling quite jolly and imagining the surprise on Donna's and Ashley's faces when they saw what Santa had left for them. It was beginning to feel a lot like Christmas, indeed.

The rest of the day was a busy one, and I decided to pull a double shift because so many other drivers were heading home to spend Christmas Eve with their families. (Back in 2003, I hadn't yet started doing my pajama visits, and so I had the night available to earn a little extra money and then spend all of Christmas Day with Linda and Ashley.) By nightfall on Christmas Eve, I had almost forgotten about the tree and wreath that I left for Donna and Ashley at their door. Then, at about 10:00 P.M., I heard the dispatcher on the radio. "Sal, you there?"

"Go ahead," I said.

"I've got the lady from Somerset on the line. She just called in. Did you drop off a tree at her place?"

"A *tree*?" I tried to sound shocked.

"Yeah, she says there was a tree outside her door when she got home, with a note saying it was for 214."

"Hmmm," I said. "Sounds like Santa visited her."

"That wasn't you?"

"Now, why would I do something like that?" I responded back into the two-way, trying to sound completely innocent.

"Hold on," I heard the dispatcher say. After a short pause, he came back on. "Okay, I told her it wasn't you, and she said she knows that it was. She was crying, and she said to tell you that no matter what you say, she'll always know it was you, and that you made Christmas magical for her and her daughter."

A rush of pure joy filled my heart. For all my years playing Santa Claus, talking to children, taking pictures, and handing out presents while wearing the red suit, I had never felt quite this wonderful before. I looked forward to returning home and telling Linda and Ashley everything that happened.

I knew before going out on my runs that Christmas Eve that it would be my last night working for the taxi company. The week before, one of my computer clients had asked me to do some work for a few weeks that would require a bit of travel on my part. At the end of my shift, I drove back to the main garage, turned in my cab and keys, collected my final paycheck, and rode off into the sunset.

About four months later, I ran into the owner of the taxi company at a local coffee shop. As we exchanged pleasantries and caught up, he told me that, right after Christmas, Donna called asking for the driver who looked like Santa Claus.

"What did you tell her?" I asked, curious to hear his answer.

"The truth," he said. "I told her that the last time I saw him was on Christmas Eve, and then he was gone. We haven't seen him since. It's really funny, but you leaving that way when you did, I guess it made her believe even more that you were the real Santa."

We laughed at how my abrupt departure on Christmas Eve just added to my Santa mystique, and I smiled as I imagined the joy of little Ashley and her mother Donna on that Christmas morning. That night, I *was* the real Santa.

✲

I KNOW I CAN'T BE A REAL-LIFE PAPÁ NOEL TO everyone out there, as much as I wish I could. But I like to think that we all have a little bit of Santa soul in us. As my family and I learned that Christmas, you don't have to wear a red velvet suit or carry a sack of toys to be Santa Claus to someone in need. If you think about it, there are hundreds of little ways and chances for us to be that shining light of hope for one another, especially during tough times. We can give money, sure, but we can also give our time, love, attention, creativity, or even just a shoulder of support. If we all looked for and acted on these opportunities, even on days that aren't Christmas, well . . . imagine the kind of world that would be.

THIRTEEN

Make a Wish

SANTA CLAUS CAN DELIVER A LOT MORE THAN just toys and gifts. You just need to know what you really want most in your heart and ask for it.

When I was a Santa-in-residence at a mall in New Hampshire, I enjoyed getting to know most of the shop owners, managers, and employees. They were a very warm and friendly bunch, and during slow periods of the day, many of them would wander over to the Santa set to hang out and chat.

One of our frequent visitors was Dennis, the assistant manager of a jewelry store on the second floor of the mall. From my big chair, I could look up and see the many sparkles of the beautiful pieces of jewelry placed in the store's window, and I would often wave at Dennis when he stepped outside into the mall atrium.

I suspected that Dennis came down to the set not so

much to visit Santa as to hang around the many attractive young ladies who worked at the North Pole Village. I'd watch Dennis flirt with some of my helpers, and I figured that a young, handsome man in his mid-twenties like Dennis had no trouble finding dates.

But apparently Dennis didn't have the kind of dating success that I had imagined. I discovered this during a Tuesday late morning lull. Dennis had come down to flirt some more with Santa's helpers, and I noticed that the young ladies did their best not to flirt back. Instead, they went about their business of cleaning the set and checking supplies. I suspected that most of these attractive helpers already had boyfriends of their own, but I can't say for sure. All I knew was that Dennis seemed pretty dejected standing there alone, despite trying to look suave and debonair in front of the giant glittered candy canes and snowmen. And so I sauntered over to him to say hello.

"Santa," he said (everyone called me Santa), letting out a bit of a frustrated sigh, "do you know what I want for Christmas—what I really want more than anything else?"

"What's that?" I asked, guessing that I already knew the answer.

"I want to find a nice girl that I can settle down with."

Yep, I was right. I gave Dennis a playful smile. "I think you have me confused with Cupid."

Dennis laughed and patted me on the shoulder. "Hey, I had to at least try to ask Santa. You never know, right?" he said. As he rode the escalator back up to the jewelry store, my heart broke a little for this poor fellow who only wanted to find love for Christmas. But it turned out that serendipity would be on Santa's side that week.

Two days later, a mother and her college-age daughter each sat on one of my knees to get a photo with Santa. After we took the picture, I asked them, "So, would you ladies like to tell me what you want for Christmas?"

The daughter immediately said with a bright look on her face, "Well, I love jewelry!"

"What's not to love?" I kidded her, and I turned to her mother. "And how about you?"

"Santa," the mother said with a tone of seriousness and loving concern in her voice, "the only thing I want for my daughter is to meet a nice gentleman and be happy."

The daughter rolled her eyes. "Mom! Really!"

Her mother just smiled. "Santa asked me what I wanted for Christmas, and that's my Christmas wish."

Hmmm . . .

"Well," I said, feeling slightly mischievous, "if you were to go up to that jewelry store over there on the second floor and ask for Dennis—and tell him that Santa sent you—well, let's just see what happens . . ."

The two ladies looked a little surprised but also intrigued, and I thought I saw them heading up in the direction of the second floor when they left. But the customer line had suddenly gotten longer, and I needed to concentrate on the children who were waiting their turn to see Santa Claus. Within a few minutes, my mind had moved on to completely different things and I forgot all about the Christmas Cupid wish.

A couple of years later, I returned to that mall in my everyday clothes to say hello to all the wonderful merchants and good friends I'd made there. I wandered in and out of stores, getting handshakes and hugs and catching up. But when I entered the jewelry store, I couldn't find Dennis anywhere. I was disappointed, as he was one of the people I'd most hoped to see.

So I asked a couple of the other shopkeepers what happened to him. I quickly learned that Dennis had been promoted and started managing a store in a different part of the state right after he got married.

"He got *married*?" I asked, surprised. "The last I knew, Dennis was still looking for a girlfriend!"

"Oh, didn't you hear? Dennis loved to tell the story of how Santa Claus introduced him to his wife."

"Really?" My ears perked up.

"Yeah. He told everyone about that day you sent a girl and her mother up to the store. Dennis and the girl hit it off immediately and started dating. Within six months, they were married, and now they've got a one-year-old daughter and another on the way."

"Well, how about that," I said, grinning from ear to ear.

So, while I can't promise anything for sure, you might as well go ahead and make that one true wish that's in your heart. In the immortal words of Dennis, "You never know, right?"

FOURTEEN

He Knows If You've Been
Bad or Good

ANOTHER WAY I SOMETIMES MADE ENDS meet in my non-Santa months was by filling in as a substitute teacher in our local school district. It gave me a chance to work with children all year long and, amusingly enough, provided me with a fun opportunity to remind them that Santa is always watching.

Imagine what might go through a student's mind when his or her substitute teacher for the day looks a lot like Santa Claus! Naturally, the reactions varied from school to school, and different age groups jumped to their conclusions in different ways. The youngest ones nearly always questioned my identity as soon as I walked in. "Are you Santa Claus?" they would always ask immediately.

"My name is Mr. Lizard," I'd answer truthfully, with a little knowing smile.

"That's a silly name!" one of the children would almost always shout out. "I think you're really Santa Claus."

"Well," I would say in a matter-of-fact tone, "if I said I was Santa Claus, how would you behave?"

They would then all reply that they'd try to be good.

"But wouldn't Santa Claus want to know how you behave when he *isn't* there?"

"Yeah," they would answer.

"So do you think Santa would tell you ahead of time that he was coming to your classroom?" I'd ask. "I bet he wouldn't! That way he could see how you behave when you don't think he's around. Does that sound about right to you?"

The kids would uniformly bob their heads in agreement.

I would then try to look thoughtful. "Hmmm . . . I doubt Santa would use his real name, though. He'd probably make one up. He'd likely come up with something fun, like an animal or something . . ."

"A lizard is an animal!" one of the smart kids would usually exclaim. "And you're Mr. *LIZARD*!"

"Yes, I am. But I didn't say I was Santa Claus," and I would smile and wink at the class. The kids would then figure out the "truth" for themselves, and usually behave extra well for Mr. Lizard.

By the time most kids reached seventh grade, few if any believed I was really Santa Claus. But one class of older kids surprised me in a big way. . . .

One day I got a call asking me to sub for a class of what they called "troubled" ninth graders. These students had difficulty focusing their attention, so teachers often struggled to keep them engaged. In fact, only the regular teacher could consistently keep these fifteen-year-olds under control, and most substitute teachers would be scheduled for just half-day shifts with these kids before being relieved by a fresh sub who hadn't yet been terrorized that day by these unruly kids.

I drove to the school to take the morning shift, and the headmaster walked me to the classroom before the students got there. He seemed to be juggling a thousand things at once and clearly wanted to set me up as quickly as possible so he could get on with the rest of the chaos of his morning.

"Here's the seating chart and class assignments for the day," he said, handing me a binder. "The kids will be here soon, and I'll check up on you occasionally. If you have a problem, we'll get somebody in here to relieve you later. But no matter what, you can't leave until I've brought in a replacement, got it?"

"Sure do," I said.

"Good luck," he said somewhat ominously. And off he went.

Just how difficult are these kids? I wondered.

The assembly bell rang, and a minute later, the doors to the classroom banged open and the students spilled in. Pandemonium reigned for a few minutes as some students found their seats while others congregated in groups talking to each other, sitting on top of desks, and playing handheld video games. I imagine the kids immediately sized me up as a substitute teacher and figured this would be an easy day to just skate by without having to do any work.

When the bell rang signaling it was time for class to start, I told everyone to sit in their assigned seats so I could take attendance. "Okay, before I call your names, it's only appropriate that I introduce myself." So I got up and wrote MR. LIZARD on the board.

"How do you pronounce that?" I heard one kid ask.

"Lizard," I said. "Just like the animal."

"You look like Santa Claus, dude!" another kid interrupted, and I heard a bunch of snickers.

"Well, for all you know, I could be," I said with my same knowing little smile.

"But you just wrote 'Mr. Lizard' up on the board!" one of the girls challenged me.

"Well, you wouldn't expect me to write 'Mr. Claus' up on the board, now, would you?"

The class laughed, and we moved on to roll call. After taking attendance, I instructed them to turn to their first assignment and start working. Teachers usually leave assignments for substitute teachers to pass out and the kids to work on quietly. But these kids were anything but quiet. I told them a few times to keep it down, but most of them went right on talking. I told them in what I hoped was a more authoritative voice to quiet down and get to work, but it had no effect. I started to get a little flustered. It was not going well.

I decided to try something. Having no idea whether it would work, I got up, walked over to the board, and wrote in large letters NAUGHTY LIST, drawing a line under it with an exaggerated flourish. Even though my back was to the class, I could sense that caught their attention. Below that, I wrote a couple of names of the kids who were talking rather than working and turned to face the class. Most of the students looked back at me, except for the ones still talking. One of the boys was chatting with a girl, and she suddenly pointed to his name written on the board.

"Hey!" he shouted indignantly as he spun around. "What are you doing?!"

I smiled slowly. "I'm used to making lists. So I figured I would share my naughty list with you. And if you're being naughty, then you're on the naughty list."

"I don't wanna be on the naughty list!" he protested.

"Well, there's only two lists you can be on, as far as I'm concerned: the naughty or the nice one."

The boy scowled, folded his arms across his chest, and slumped down angrily into his seat.

In my heart, I believe Santa Claus *wants* kids to be

on the nice list, so I prompted the class with an unspo-
ken promise, "But you all know the song, dontcha?
'He's making a list, and . . .' " I waited.

". . . checking it twice," the entire class said together.

"Exactly!" I waved my arm in acknowledgment of
the correct answer. "So if you stop being naughty, then
you'll probably get back on the nice list." And I went
over to the other side of the board and wrote NICE LIST
with a line underneath.

Amazingly, the kids quieted down, and most of them
opened their books. When I noticed students quietly
doing their assignment (instead of filing their nails
or staring off into space), I would write their names on
the nice list. Students who ignored the assignment or
acted up went onto the naughty list. And if one of the
students who was on the naughty list quieted down
and got cracking on their work, I would move their
name from the naughty to nice list. As the morning
went on, more and more names migrated in the right
direction.

I had been there for about two hours when the headmaster finally walked in to check on me. The kids all
sat diligently doing their work, and the headmaster appeared totally shocked. He looked around the classroom and then turned to me with an expression of total
disbelief on his face. "I can't believe how quiet and engaged they are!"

"Well, the teacher left a lot of work for them to do," I said.

"But they never actually *do it*," the headmaster said. He scratched his head, looking confounded, but he quickly got himself focused again. "So, are you going to need to be relieved at noon?"

"Oh, no," I replied with a warm smile. "Everything's just fine here. I'm happy to finish out the day."

The headmaster now seemed completely confused. I don't think that he'd ever had a substitute teacher in such good spirits after two hours with these kids. "Well, um, great then." He started to leave but stopped as he opened the door. "What's your secret? How did you get them to do their work?"

I pointed to the board over my shoulder and said, "Nobody wants to be on the naughty list."

His face took on a sarcastic expression. "Oh, yeah, like you're Santa!" He turned around, shaking his head, and walked out.

The kids all looked up at me, and I said, "See? Some folks just don't believe." And I added in a low whisper, "Ho, ho, ho."

The students behaved for the rest of the day, finishing all their work and remaining mostly quiet. These teenagers probably hadn't believed in Santa for many years, but I think they wanted to hedge their bets, just in case. Santa's lists of naughty and nice may be the stuff of legend, but from what I've seen, when Santa Claus is around, nobody wants to take any chances.

As I packed up the kids' completed assignments at the end of the day, I smiled thinking about how much the lore of Santa Claus motivates us to behave admirably—whether we're five, fifteen, or fifty years old. I turned off the classroom light, closed the door, and walked to my car softly whistling to myself.

"So be good for goodness' sake . . ."

FIFTEEN

Won't You Guide My Sleigh Tonight?

I THINK ONE OF THE NICEST PARTS OF CHRIST-
mas is that it offers the promise of renewal. Maybe
it's because it comes so close to the end of the year, or
because of the sense of goodwill and compassion in the
air. But no matter what inspires it, Christmas is a time
for forgiveness and hope. On one fateful night, this
Santa actually steered his "sleigh" through a Christmastime blizzard to make sure one family got the message
that there's always the possibility for second chances.

❄

EVERY YEAR, THE SAME THING HAPPENS. THE
closer it gets to Christmas, the more last-minute calls

come in requesting Santa appearances. While I'd love to accommodate every request, and I try to fit in as many visits as I can each season, I invariably have to turn down many of the people who wait until the days just before Christmas to call me. And so it happened during the second week of December 2008 that I received a phone call asking for another last-minute Santa visit.

"Is this the Genuine Santa?" the woman's voice asked, referring to the name of my website, GenuineSanta.com.

"Ho, ho, ho! That's me!" I said in a jolly voice. "What can I do for you?"

"How much do you charge for a visit?"

I usually find that when folks lead with that question, it's because money is a concern. So I always respond in such a way that gives them the dignity of having choices without embarrassing them. "Well, it all depends on a lot of things," I said matter-of-factly. "If I have any openings left during the time that you want me to come, if it's a day or evening visit, weekday or weekend, how many children will there be, and so on. Can you give me a little more information about the visit?" I was frankly doubtful that I could fit in any more visits this late in the season, but I didn't want to outright turn her away.

"Well," she said, her voice starting to quiver a little. "It's for my son. He's in a children's home. He's been taken away from me by the state, but I'm gonna get him back one day, I swear. I'm in a twelve-step program, and I'm working really hard. But they won't let me see him, not even for Christmas, and it's so hard being alone—for him and for me."

Any feeling of doubt I had vanished completely, instantly replaced by overwhelming sympathy. I thought about how difficult it was for Linda and me having Ashley—by then a grown young woman out on her own—so far away from us at Christmastime. "Oh, my gosh, I'm so sorry . . ."

"It's okay," the woman said. "I know I screwed up. I started drinking after my divorce, and they were right to take Zachary away from me. He's such a good boy, and he deserves a sober mom. I love him so much, and I just want him to know that he's not alone on Christmas."

I could hear the sincerity and pain in her voice. I personally believe that most people out there don't have a malicious bone in their body. They just screw up sometimes and make bad choices or frustrating mistakes, for many and varied reasons. I try not to judge people because unless you've been where they are, you can't know that you wouldn't make the wrong choices, too.

I believe that everyone deserves a second chance to get things right, and I have to believe that Santa feels the same way. No one *wants* to be naughty. They just went off track somewhere along the way. Santa offers us a reminder of the ever-present opportunity to move to the nice list at any time simply by doing and being good.

So there was no question of what I would do next. "I can make an appearance at the home where your son is living," I told her. I figured I could probably fit it in between a few other of my local visits set up for that week.

"Oh, that would be wonderful!" she exclaimed. "And I'd like you to please give him a special present from me."

"How many children are there in the home?" I asked.

"About twelve, I think."

"Will there be presents for the other children, too?"

"No, I can't really afford to get gifts for all of them," she said. "It'll just be one for Zachary from his mommy being delivered by Santa Claus."

I immediately saw the problem with this plan. "Ma'am, Santa Claus would never visit a houseful of children and give a Christmas present to only one of them. I'd need to have enough gifts to give every child."

I could hear her becoming disheartened. "But that'll be much more than I can afford."

"Oh, they don't have to be elaborate, expensive presents," I assured her. "You can get fun little toys and games for under five dollars at most stores. I hand out those sorts of things all the time. I tell the children they're 'holdover presents' for being extra good, and they're just to keep things fun while waiting for the big presents on Christmas Day itself."

The woman sounded more hopeful. "Well, maybe I could afford to do it that way."

I flashed back to how wonderful my family and I felt that year we extended ourselves to Donna and her daughter, who didn't have presents or a tree, and I was inspired to help this woman any way I could. "I'll tell you what: if you supply enough toys for all the children and set it up with the home, I'll deduct the cost of the toys from my fee. Then you won't be paying any extra."

"Really?" she asked, truly surprised.

"As long as you make sure all the presents are just about the same price range. I don't want to give out eleven water pistols and yo-yos and then hand Zachary a microscope. It wouldn't be right. But I can give Zachary a special message from you by whispering in his ear while he's sitting on my lap. That way, the other children won't know that he's been singled out."

The woman seemed extremely happy with the idea and told me she'd go set up the visit with the children's home and call me back. The following day, however, her voice on the telephone sounded defeated and hopeless. "Mr. Lizard," she said quietly, "I'm so sorry to have troubled you. But I can't afford to do this. Please accept my apologies."

What would Santa do?

"Okay," I said without hesitation, "how about if I don't charge you anything for my visit? I'll just show up at the home. Can you still supply me with the toys to hand out?"

At first she sounded unsure. "Um, yes, I think so." Then, because I think she didn't quite understand me and wanted to be certain of what I'd just said, she asked, "You mean you won't charge me *anything*?"

"If you can go out and buy the toys, yes, then I'll happily do the visit for free."

"Yes! Oh, certainly, yes! Oh, thank you so much! I can get you the toys. Are you sure you don't mind?"

I laughed. "Ma'am, I'm Santa Claus. It's what I do."

The woman called the children's home, and, after I had a brief phone interview with them and the folks at the home ran a quick background check, they cleared me for a visit. Meanwhile, the woman went out to a local toy store and bought a dozen five-dollar toys for me to hand out. Unfortunately, she couldn't drop them off with me because her driver's license had been suspended. But in for a penny, in for a pound, I drove an hour to her home to pick up the gifts for the children.

"I don't know how I can ever thank you," she said at the door.

"You just keep working hard to get your son back," I told her. "Now, I'll need to get the address of the children's home."

"Oh, yes. Let me write it down for you." She grabbed

a pen and paper, scribbled out an address, and handed it to me.

I looked at the address in shock. "Wow," I said, before I could even stop the word from escaping my mouth. I'd assumed the children's home would be close to this woman's house so I could fit the visit in between others, and that the mileage costs wouldn't be significant for me. But it wasn't close at all.

"What is it?" she asked nervously. "What's wrong?"

"Well, this address is a two-hour drive for me in the other direction, and . . ."

I could see the hope fading from her eyes. *What would Santa do?*

". . . and you know what? Don't worry about it. I'll take care of it."

Tears began filling her eyes. She went to hug me. "Thank you. Oh, thank you so much!"

I hugged her back, and then I wished her luck and told her I hoped things would work out for her. "I promise to give Zachary your message," I said as I got into my van.

Early the next morning, snow started falling . . . and falling . . . and falling. More than two inches of snow *per hour* blanketed the ground, blown by forty-five-mile-per-hour gusts that created bitterly cold wind chills and reduced visibility on most roadways to zero. Such treacherous weather conditions resulted in the authorities issuing a "Level 3 Snow Emergency." The strongest road travel advisory that can be issued, a Level 3 Snow Emergency states that "All roadways are closed to non-emergency personnel. No one should be out during these conditions unless it is absolutely necessary to travel. . . . Those traveling on the roadways may subject themselves to arrest."

Very bad timing for me.

My appearance at the children's home had been scheduled for that afternoon, smack dab in the middle of the worst part of this major winter storm. With only a week until Christmas, I had no openings left to reschedule. And more than that, the children had been told to expect a visit from Santa Claus. And when has a blizzard ever stopped the big man in the red suit from showing up?

I knew I had to get myself there somehow. So I put on my Santa outfit, got into my van, and left extra early to give myself enough time to travel there through the storm.

The driving conditions deteriorated quickly as I turned onto the interstate. Fortunately, I had snow tires and a significant amount of experience driving through severe winter conditions—snow, sleet, ice, blizzards, you name it. I'd lived and worked in New England through nearly a decade of tough winters. Even so, I found that drive to be one of the most difficult of my life. Although I literally saw no other cars on the highway— since everyone else seemed to have obeyed the emergency advisory—I still had to keep my speed down, and a few times I even had to pull over to stop and wait for a snow squall to clear and allow me to see again.

By the time I'd made it about halfway, the snow had decreased visibility so much that I heard the police siren behind me long before I could see the flashing red and blue lights in my rearview mirror. I signaled to indicate that I'd pull over as soon as I could safely do so, and a few moments later, I came to a stop along the shoulder of the interstate.

I could see the state trooper, bundled in a thick gray and blue coat, get out of his patrol car and walk toward my vehicle. I rolled down my window, and snow immediately blew in. Fortunately, I was bundled up myself in full, ultra-warm Santa Claus regalia.

The state trooper looked into the van. "Where are you going, Santa?" he asked, obviously noticing my costume.

"I'm on my way to a children's home to deliver Christmas presents to some boys and girls there."

"You realize that during a Level 3 Snow Emergency, it's emergency vehicles only allowed on the roads. So why shouldn't I cite you?"

I spread out my arms to show my entire outfit. "Officer, look at me." I smiled. "I'm the one person in the world who can't use snow as an excuse not to show up. And anyway, this is a children's home. It's not like the boys and girls won't be able to make it there because of the snow. They live there, and they're expecting Santa to come this afternoon. I just can't bear to disappoint children, especially at this time of year."

The officer thought about it for a moment. "Okay, you've got a point. But I can't have you risking your life driving alone in these conditions. So I'll tell you what: I'll drive along in front of you until you get there. You all right with that, Santa?"

"Oh, that would be just great!" I responded happily. "There's nothing like getting a police escort."

The irony was not lost on me as I steered through that stormy night, a glowing red light up ahead of me guiding the way. We slowly and carefully drove the remaining distance and pulled into the parking lot of the children's home. It was a friendly looking two-story house with lots of windows, a porch, and a front door with small panels of stained glass. The officer got out of his vehicle and walked over to me as I headed toward the front door.

"Hey, Santa, wait a sec," he said. "Would you mind if I came inside with you? I'd love to see the expression on the kids' faces when they see you."

"How about this?" I said. "Why don't you go in first? Then you can introduce me."

"I'd really enjoy that, thanks!" he said, grinning. So I stood back a little and waited for him to ring the doorbell. When the door opened, I could see a bunch of children inside, all looking for Santa. They seemed surprised and disappointed to see a policeman instead. The officer took a step inside but kept the door propped just a crack so he could open it and let me in. I tiptoed up to listen to his introduction.

"Wow! There's quite a storm outside!" the officer said loudly. "In fact, there's a Level 3 Snow Emergency! Do any of you kids know what that is?" I heard a bunch of quiet mumbles. "Well, it's when a blizzard is so bad that only police cars and fire trucks are allowed to be on the roads. No one else is allowed to drive right now. In fact, if I saw somebody out driving in this storm, I could arrest them."

I heard a lot of children saying "Wow!" and muttering after he said that. When the voices faded, the officer continued. "But then I saw someone who's allowed to be out in a Level 3 Snow Emergency because he's so important. And I followed him here. I think you already know who I'm talking about . . ."

He opened the door wide, and I walked in with a loud, "Ho, ho, ho! Merry Christmas!" The children cheered and ran to hug me, yelling "Santa! Santa! Santa!"

The officer stayed for a few minutes, asking the folks in charge if they might need anything, and then he headed back out to continue patrolling the highways. The children all said good-bye, and then we sang some songs and I told a few stories (including the story of Rudolph the Red-Nosed Reindeer, of course).

I handed out the small gift toys, and then one by one,

the children climbed onto my lap to have pictures taken and talk to Santa. Zachary's mother had shown me a photo of her son the previous day, and when he climbed up onto my lap, I said, "And you must be Zachary!"

Zachary told me he'd been good and how he made a lot of friends living there in the children's home. Then he eagerly listed all the toys he wanted for Christmas. "But I really wish I could see my mom," he said, suddenly looking a little sad.

"Well, Zachary," I confided, leaning over to whisper into his ear. "Your mother actually gave me a special message to share with you when I came here, but don't tell anyone else, okay?"

Zachary looked excited. "Okay, Santa! What did she say?"

"Your mom told me that she loves you very, very much. She knows you're such a good boy, and she's trying really hard to get you back. And she'll never stop trying. You've just got to keep believing in her."

Zachary gave me a big hug and a smile. I smiled back as he got down off my lap.

By the time I'd finished with the last child, one of the grown-ups told me that the worst of the storm had passed and that the authorities had opened the roads again.

As I turned to say good-bye to all of the children, I left them with one final thought. "I want you all to remember something very important, all right?" The children nodded as they paid careful attention. "Even though you're in this particular situation right now, you all need to know that you're loved—each of you. You're not being punished. You see, Santa knows a secret, and I'll share it with all of you right now. Ready?"

Again, the children nodded and listened closely. "There's no such thing as a bad child or parent. There's only bad behavior. Everyone gets onto Santa's naughty list at least once. Sometimes it's a lot of times. That's just the way people are. Children make mistakes, and— believe it or not—sometimes grown-ups and parents make mistakes, too. But that doesn't mean that they're bad. Santa knows that people are good, and they have to be given a second chance. And that's why I always make it a point to check my list twice. There's always hope. Things might not be perfect right now, but there's always a chance they'll get better, maybe even in ways you never imagined . . . you just have to believe."

And with that, I wished everyone a Merry Christmas and headed out into the chilly winter night.

SIXTEEN

A Santa for All Ages

WHILE I MAY NOT HAVE SET OUT AT FIRST
to become Santa Claus, I've lived many magical moments since that serendipitous day in Charleston
that have turned me into a lifelong believer in the spirit
of Christmas. I've seen twinkles of joy in countless children's eyes and more Christmas miracles than any man
should expect to in one lifetime. I've witnessed the res-
toration of faith in grown-ups who considered themselves too old or disenchanted to believe, and I've had
my own heart healed and uplifted again and again
through the mysterious power of the red suit.

I remember so many of the folks I've met along the
way who made my life as Santa inspiring and fun. But
no one has ever embodied the indomitable spirit of loving both Santa Claus and Christmas quite like Lottie.

During one season as Santa-in-residence at a mall in

New England, it was nearing Christmas Day, and the lines to see Santa Claus had grown very long. People waited hours just to take their photo with Santa, and so I was a little surprised and certainly impressed to see a woman of fairly advanced years walk up the carpet to my chair. But the long wait standing in line didn't seem to have affected her, and she hopped right up, threw both her legs sideways across my lap, and put her arms around me.

"So what's your name, little girl?" I asked mischievously.

She smiled and said, "I'm Lottie. And I'll have you know that I've had my picture taken with Santa Claus each year since before I was born."

"Ho, ho, ho!" I laughed. "Since *before* you were born? And how did you manage that, Lottie?"

"I have a photo of my mother, pregnant with me, sitting on Santa's lap with his ear pressed up to her belly, listening to my Christmas wish from inside the womb. Then each year from then forward, I had my picture taken with Santa Claus. First it was just me. Then it was me and my brother, and then me and my two brothers.

"By the time I was in high school, my brothers wouldn't take their picture with Santa anymore. But I still did. Then, when I went away to college, that first year I had my picture taken with Santa, and I sent it to my mother. The following year, I took my Santa picture with my first-ever boyfriend. The year after that, I had my picture taken with a different boyfriend."

She gave me a smile and a wink, and I smiled back, wanting to hear more of her story.

"Later on, I took pictures of Santa with me and my husband, then with our children in them, too. When the last of our children moved away, I went back to taking pictures with just me and my husband.

"Then my husband passed away. But by that point, there started to be grandchildren who would come to visit, so I would take my Santa Claus photos with them."

"And you still have all of these pictures?" I asked, amazed.

"Oh, yes," she said. "Every one from the womb on through last Christmas. In fact, I was showing them all to my daughters, who were trying to figure out what to do for my eightieth birthday, which is coming up right after Christmas. They've decided to have all the photos enlarged, framed, and hung on the walls at my party, and then put them into a special bound book. They're going to call it 'My Lifelong Affair with Santa Claus.' So I need a special picture this year."

And with that, she raised up her right hand to cup my beard and leaned in to kiss me on the cheek. The photographer snapped off several photos in that pose, and then Lottie got up and thanked me, telling me that this photo would be on the cover of the book her daughters were making.

"I plan to live a long time," she said. "So every ten years after this, we're going to rebind the book with the next ten photos for everyone in the family."

"That's such a wonderful legacy for your children and grandchildren," I said, truly impressed and inspired by this woman whom I had met only a few short minutes before.

She grinned. "And I intend to keep doing it as long as this old body can still get out here to the mall to see you."

"Lottie," I said quietly, "I want to give you something." I leaned over and asked one of the helpers to get me one of my business cards, and I handed it to her. "I'm sure you're going to live a lot more years," I whispered into her ear, "but if it's ever Christmastime and you find that you're too sick to come see me, give me a call, and I'll come to see you. It doesn't matter where you are; I'll get there. If you're in a hospital, I'll come right up to your room and take a picture with you by your bed. All you have to do is call me."

I feel incredibly grateful to have met folks like Lottie during my life as Santa. They've made me as happy as the real Santa Claus could ever hope to be. Every time that I have a Santa Claus encounter, whenever someone recognizes me, reaches out to me with a friendly greeting, handshake, or hug, or simply gives me a smile, it reminds me that the spirit of Christmas can be held in your heart at any age and on any day of the year.

I've learned firsthand that Christmas is magic—pure

and simple. It remains the one holiday when people will go out of their way to be extra nice and generous to others. It is a chance for us to put the stress of everyday life on hold for just a bit and celebrate all the joys and inherent goodness of humanity. Christmas reminds us of happy memories and big wishes for the future that might just come true. All we need to do is believe, and keep our eyes and hearts open for those unmistakable flashes of Christmas magic that show up whether we're eight years old or eighty.

So far, Lottie hasn't called me. But if and when she ever does, I fully intend to keep my promise to come to her bedside for a photo—no matter how far I have to travel.

After all, that's what Santa would do.

ACKNOWLEDGMENTS

Sal would like to thank . . .

Jonathan Lane, my collaborator on this book—While I might be an entertaining storyteller, Jonathan is a true wordsmith. We worked together for more than two years on this wonderful book, recording more than fifty hours of telephone interviews and drilling down into the vaults of my memory until every important detail had been unearthed for Jonathan to organize and write up with me. I can honestly say that without Jonathan involved, this book would never have gotten written.

Linda Lizard, my wife—It's not easy being married to Santa Claus. Each Christmas season, her husband all but disappears for two or three months. And I'm also away from home at other times during the year, leaving poor Linda to manage the home front all by herself. It's been challenging at times, and I don't take the time to thank Linda for her patience, understanding, and support nearly enough. So I want to use this opportunity to put it down in writing for all to see. Thank you, Linda. I love you, too.

Jonathan would like to thank . . .

Sal Lizard, the world's best Santa Claus—When I first heard some of Sal's Santa stories, I said, "You need to write a book!" Although Sal had thought about such a project, he tended to get really busy and hadn't really gotten anywhere. So I said, "Hey, maybe I could help you write it!" What followed was a two-year odyssey during which I learned so many incredible things about this truly inspirational man, and we developed a close connection—even across three thousand miles—a friendship that I've come to cherish. Sal has an amazing memory, and I continue to marvel at all he's experienced and accomplished in his life.

William B. Stanford, my father-in-law—A first-time author like myself, my father-in-law inspired me by writing his own book and getting it published. In his case, the book was about the amazing life his parents had experienced in France during World War II (it's called *Lizzi and Fredl: A Perilous Journey of Love and Faith*, and it's a must-read). William spent years interviewing his parents and turning their stories into an engrossing manuscript. He then managed to find a publisher and get his book into stores, proving to me and others that even a novice, unpublished author can still make it to the big time.

Dedee Lane, my mother—A teacher of reading and English for nearly fifty years, Mom was my first editor. She pushed me to delve ever deeper into Sal's thoughts and feelings to provide more emotional insight into his stories and enrich the reading experience. Mom caught more typos than I could ever count and, along with my father, Arthur, played cheerleader through what was a roller-coaster ride on the road to publication. They never stopped believing in Santa and also in Sal and me.

Wendy Lane, my wife—Each day as I wrote this book, Wendy headed off to a very demanding job while I stayed home and took care of our brand-new son, Jayden. She would have so loved to spend more time with Jayden, and maybe, if this book is successful, that can still happen. In the meantime, though, I see Wendy's dedication and hard work, and I know that I can never thank her enough for the sacrifices she makes each and every day of our lives together with our beautiful son. I love you so much, honey.

Sal and Jonathan together would like to thank . . .

Scott Waxman, our literary agent—As first-time authors, neither of us had any clue how this whole process works. Scott was very patient, professional, and always friendly and helpful at every step of the way. We couldn't have asked for a better agent to represent us.

Jessica Sindler, our editor—Not knowing what to expect after finding a publisher for our book, we felt a little nervous going into the editorial process. But our editor was as nice as nice could be, a true joy to work with. We learned that editors strive to make a book come out perfectly, and Jessica's suggestions were spot-on. We love our editor!

Debra Goldstein, industry veteran—The waters of professional publication can be unpredictable and, at times, even treacherous, especially to novices like us. Deb brought her many years of knowledge and experience to help guide our manuscript to a safe harbor and bring this wonderful book to all of you. We couldn't have done it without you, Deb.

The entire Gotham publishing team—From president William Shinker to the marketing and publicity teams, everyone has been so wonderful to us. They all believe in Santa Claus, and they believe in our book. We're so honored to have such a great publishing company to help bring *Being Santa Claus* to Christmas enthusiasts everywhere.

The more than four thousand members of STAR-FLEET, the International Star Trek *Fan Association*—Yes, Santa is a Trekkie, and so is his cowriter. In fact, that's how we met. Sal was president of the STAR-FLEET International fan club, serving a three-year term, and Jonathan was his chief of communications. Both Sal and Jonathan have spent decades in this wonderful organization, developing close friendships and having lots of fun. So we wanted to make sure our beloved fan club got mentioned somewhere in this book. And if you know a *Star Trek* fan out there somewhere, send them to www.sfi.org to sign up.

ABOUT THE AUTHORS

SAL LIZARD has been playing Santa Claus profession-
ally for more than twenty years. He lives in Georgia
with his wife, Linda (aka Mrs. Claus).

JONATHAN LANE has worked as both a teacher and, before that, as a creative director for Nestlé's Willy Wonka
website, Wonka.com. Jonathan lives in Southern Cali-
fornia with his wife and son.